A WILTSHIRE RAILWAY REMEMBERED
The Devizes Branch

1. A 'Hall' class 4-6-0 emerges from Devizes tunnel with a Trowbridge-Reading train, 11 May 1963. (P. Strong)

Nigel S. M. Bray

1984
PICTON PUBLISHING
CHIPPENHAM · WILTS

DB-A

Photoset in $8\frac{1}{2}$ on 11 pt Century Schoolbook
Text paper supplied by Howard Smith Papers, Bristol.
Bound by J. W. Braithwaite & Son Ltd, Wolverhampton.
Printed in Great Britain by Picton Print
Citadel Works, Bath Road, Chippenham, Wiltshire.
PP45593

Author's Note

My interest in the Devizes line arises from my grandfather, Sidney Bray, having been Devizes Station Master from 1948 to 1953. It has been a pleasure to meet people who worked with him during that period, and who have assisted me in my research.

I myself joined British Rail in 1976, and am currently working in the Regional Headquarters offices at Swindon.

ACKNOWLEDGEMENTS

Thanks are due to the staff of Wiltshire County Libraries; Wiltshire County Record Office; the Public Record Office at Kew; and Mrs P. Colman, Librarian of the Wiltshire Archaeological & Natural History Society.

I would like to make a special mention of Paul Strong and Peter Weston for guiding my research in the first instance, and not least Joy Turner for typing the manuscript and suggesting a number of improvements.

Grateful acknowledgement for their assistance is due to: K. G. Baker, A. Bamfield, Miss K. Bishop, S. P. J. A. Derek, W. A. Fitton, T. J. Gaylard, Mr and Mrs J. Giddings, W. J. Griffin, M. E. Hatch, A. J. Horner, G. R. Hounsell, A. Mead, M. C. Obst, R. G. Reynolds, A. J. Scown, Mrs P. Strong, Mr and Mrs P. Topp, J. W. Tottle, V. Tucker, D. J. B. Turner, C. Wake, C. F. D. Whetmath.

Nigel S. M. Bray
February 1984

Contents

List of Illustrations

20. 3735 in the loop platform at Patney with the 11.35 am stopper to Westbury via Devizes, January 1961. (P. Strong)

21. 0-6-0PT 9628 shunts Devizes up yard, c1959. (P. Strong)

22. 11.35 am train to Devizes leaving Patney, formed by a single railcar, January 1960. This working later reverted to steam haulage. (P. Strong)

23. *Rhuddlan Castle* climbs away from Pans Lane Halt towards Patney. Note the two vans for parcels. (P. Strong)

24. 4950 *Patshull Hall* on a Trowbridge–Reading train climbing Caen Hill bank, 1962. (P. Strong)

25. The 11.35 train leaving Patney for Westbury via Devizes, January 1961. The double track in the foreground is the main Lavington line to Westbury. (P. Strong)

26. 6959 *Peatling Hall* approaches Devizes with a Trowbridge–Paddington train. (P. Strong)

27. A two-car DMU on the branch at Stert Junction. (P. Strong)

28. A 9F 2-10-0 prepares to leave Devizes with the 23.30 Hoo Junction cement train. (P. Strong)

29. D7040 on the 07.10 Trowbridge–Paddington train entering Devizes where a 9F 2-10-0 waits with the down cement train. (P. Strong)

30. A DMU finds little custom at Seend, c1965. (P. Strong)

31. Seend station after removal of the goods yard. (P. Strong)

32. 4472 *Flying Scotsman* visiting the line on 19 October 1963 with a Paddington–Ilfracombe excursion. (P. Strong)

33. 3735 hauls the down pick up goods towards Patney at Stert, summer 1963. (P. Strong)

34. Pick-up goods between Devizes and Patney, c1963. (P. Strong)

35. Pick-up goods train in the south face of the island platform, 1964. Devizes shunter Joe Giddings is second from right. (P. Strong)

36. Trowbridge–Paddington train crosses the morning commuter train to Westbury at Devizes, spring 1965. (P. Strong)

37. Signalman Bert Clack throws the Devizes–Holt token to the driver of the 18.30 train to Westbury, June 1965. (P. Strong)

38. A DMU waits to depart from Devizes on the last day of service, 16 April 1966. (P. Strong)

39. DMU entering Devizes on the last day of operation, 16 April 1966. (P. Strong)

40, 41, & 42. Devizes station shortly after closure. (P. Strong)

43. D809 *Champion* at Devizes with demolition train, March 1967. (P. Strong)

44. Demolition contractor's loco at Devizes, March 1967. (P. Strong)

45. Demolition train at Devizes, March 1967. (P. Strong)

46. The end of the line. Lifting in progress between Patney and Devizes, March 1967. (P. Strong)

47. The junction at Holt, April 1966. The Devizes branch curves to the right. (P. Strong)

48. Semington Halt, looking east. (Lens of Sutton)

49. 5416 prepares to run round before returning to Westbury with a passenger train one May evening in 1959. Note wooden signal posts. (P. Strong)

50. A 'Hall' class loco prepares to leave Devizes with the Sunday lunchtime train to Westbury (ex-Reading), c1960. (P. Strong)

51. Seend station after removal of the platform loop, looking east. (P. Strong)

52. Bromham & Rowde Halt, the sawmill is in the right background. (Lens of Sutton)

53. A 'Hall' crosses Foxhangers Bridge with an up train. (P. Strong)

54. A 'Hall' 4-6-0 takes a Trowbridge–Reading train up Caen Hill bank, 1962. (P. Strong)

55. 5940 *Whitbourne Hall* reaches the summit of the incline. Note the board 'All down goods and mineral trains to stop dead here'. (P. Strong)

56. Devizes station looking west. (Lens of Sutton)

57. Forecourt of Devizes station during demolition, March 1967. (P. Strong)

58. Devizes station looking east. (Lens of Sutton)

59. Devizes station looking west. (P. Strong)

60. Devizes signalbox. (P. Strong)

61. Devizes station, west end showing water crane on island platform. (P. Strong)

62. Pans Lane Halt, looking east. (Lens of Sutton)

63. Patney & Chirton, looking west, between the wars. (Mowat Collection)

64. Patney & Chirton, looking east, about 1920. (Mowat Collection)

65. Patney signalbox, shortly after closure. (P. Strong)

66. Wirral Railway Circle railtour pauses at site of Holt Junction, 27 March 1971. (G. R. Hounsell)

67. Enthusiasts inspect the site of Holt Junction, 27 March 1971. The remains of the Devizes branch curves away to the right; note the wagons stored on it. (G. R. Hounsell)

68. Poster advertising a Newbury Race Special routed via Devizes, 1926.

69. Troop train entering Devizes, probably during World War One, hauled by Midland & South Western Junction Railway 4-4-0 No. 7. (P. Strong Collection)

ONE

The Reluctant Great Western

In the 1830s, Devizes, a flourishing market town widely regarded as the logical centre of Wiltshire, took pains to get involved in proposals for a railway between London and Bristol. Local businessmen, dissatisfied with the slowness of barge transport along the Kennet & Avon Canal, had high hopes of a rail link. A prospectus for a 'Bristol & London Railway' via Bradford-on-Avon, Devizes, Hungerford and Reading, was issued from an address in Lombard Street, London in May 1832 but the scheme appears to have died in 1833 through lack of capital.[1]

A severe setback for local hopes came in 1834 when the Great Western Railway's proposed London–Bristol line put forward a route between Reading and Bath which went north of the Marlborough Downs instead. Brunel, appointed as project engineer in 1833, had rejected a route via Pewsey Vale and Devizes in favour of one via Swindon because the latter line would have easier gradients and allow for expansion of the system to the Midlands and South Wales.

Devizes was not consoled by the GWR's talk of 'probable branches' to Bradford and Trowbridge. Local interests looked favourably on the rival scheme of the London & Southampton Railway (later the London & South Western Railway) for a line to Bristol from Basingstoke via Newbury, Hungerford, Devizes and Trowbridge.

The GWR retaliated by announcing that their Chippenham–Trowbridge/Bradford branch was now a definite proposal; Brunel humiliated the LSR Directors at their public meeting in Bath in September 1834 by astute questioning, which won a resolution there and then in support of the GWR schemes. Despite this weakening of support at Bath for the LSR scheme, intermediate towns such as Devizes remained in favour of it and both companies proceeded with their Parliamentary Bills.

The House of Commons Committee examining the rival proposals was chaired by Charles Russell, MP for Reading (a town directly on the GWR route), and who was later to become the Great Western's Chairman. The easier gradients of Brunel's route commended it to the Committee. Russell ridiculed the LSR's argument that, although their 'Bath and Basing' route was less level than the GWR's its gradients were so balanced as to make it 'practically level'. He replied that on that line of argument the Scottish Highlands would be ideal for railway construction. When both Bills were considered by the Lords in 1835 the GWR, whose technical witnesses outclassed their opponents, were victorious.

A group of Devizes citizens made the most of this setback by engaging Brunel to survey a route for a branch to Melksham, itself on the GWR's projected branch from Chippenham. The proposed line started from a triangular junction at Melksham. After crossing the K&A Canal at Sells Green two alternative lines were surveyed to a terminus in the Market Place; level crossings were on the more northerly of

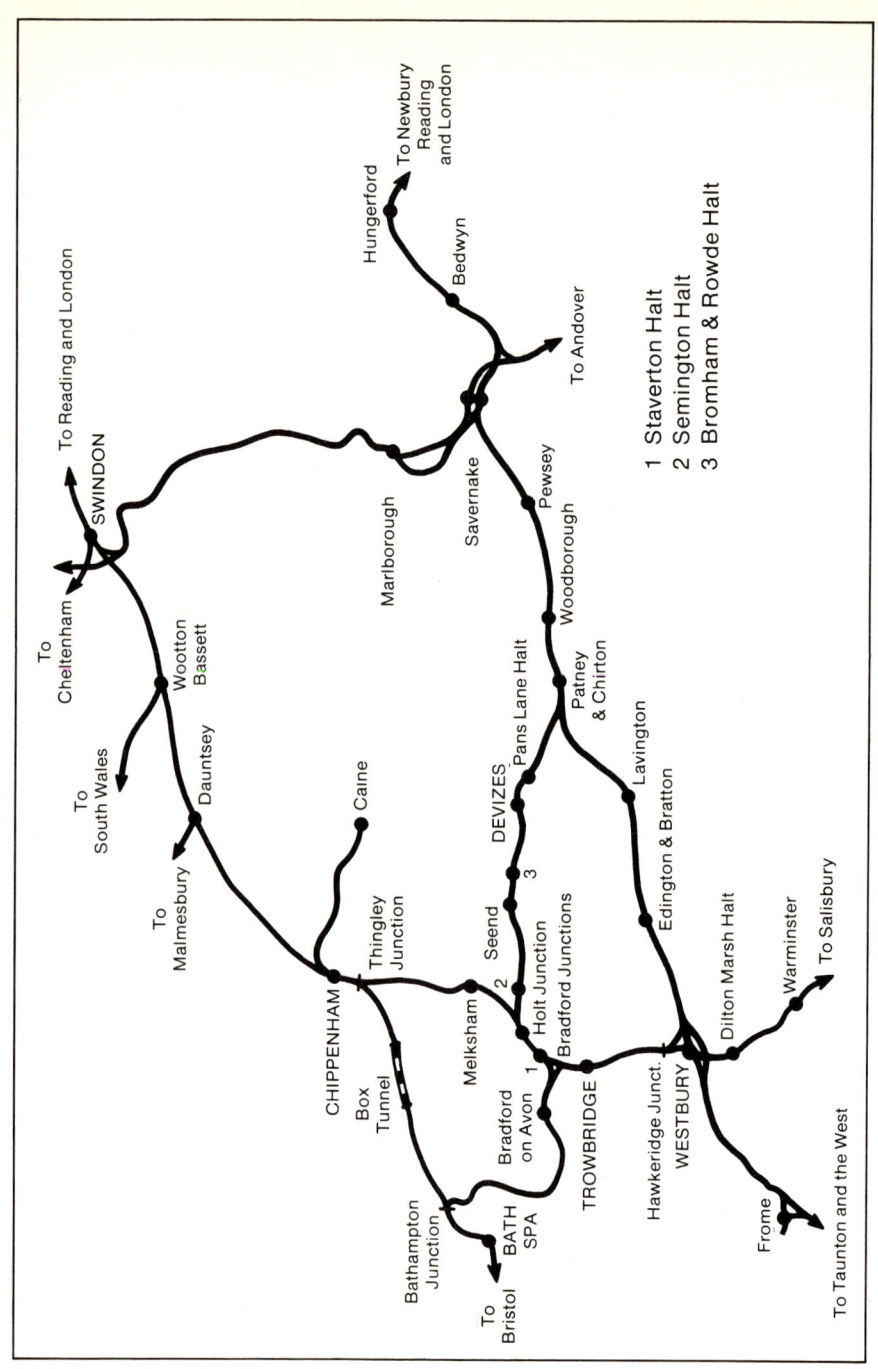

2. The Devizes Branch and related lines.

these as well as at Red Stocks Lane and Praters Lane on the common section north of Sells Green. A meeting to launch the 'Devizes & Melksham Great Western Union Railway' on 2 July 1836 at the Bear Hotel in Devizes, allotted shares but no further progress appears to have been made.

A possible explanation is that leading citizens still pinned their hopes on railway schemes that placed Devizes on a direct route to London and Bristol. But a public meeting in May 1844 chaired by the Mayor voted overwhelmingly in favour of the 1836 Devizes & Melksham scheme. Brunel was among the GWR officers present; his colleague Hayter referred to 'a great desire' on the part of Devizes to be connected to the GWR when it was first incorporated but said earlier proposals had not materialised. It seems reasonable to assume that the GWR Directors wanted to placate Devizes, lest the town support rival schemes which might keep them out of West Wiltshire, Somerset and Dorset altogether. That Company naturally wanted people from Devizes to support its designs in those counties. The GWR formulated the Wiltshire & Somerset Railway Company at a meeting in Warminster on 9 July 1844, and it was renamed the Wilts, Somerset & Weymouth Railway Company in October.

At the meeting Brunel presented plans for a network leaving the GWR main line at Thingley, west of Chippenham and including a Melksham-Devizes branch. The Company appointed bankers and solicitors in the principal towns. In Devizes, Messrs Hughes, Lock & Co were its bankers, Messrs Tugwell & Meek, solicitors. John Saunders produced estimates of likely revenue, based partly on existing coach traffic. He assumed that rail travel would attract enough additional custom to double his total predicted passenger revenue of £20,104 0s 0d per year which included £374 8s 0d from passengers then using the Devizes-Bath stage coaches, and £608 8s 0d from then users of the Bath-Devizes-Reading Star Coach. These calculations were based on rail fares of 2d per mile for an average railway distance of 12 or 13 miles, multiplied by the annual total of coach passengers. In other words, the Wilts & Somerset expected to kill these coach routes.

Saunders predicted that 'Devizes and vicinity' would bring the railway an annual income from various sources as under:

£1,083 0s 0d from 5,000 tons of light goods.
£704 0s 0d from 6,500 tons of corn.
£379 0s 0d from 3,500 tons of heavy goods.
£1,725 0s 0d from 9,000 tons of coal.

Most of the Devizes freight estimates were calculated on an average rail distance of 13 miles, 2d per ton per mile (4d in the case of light goods), but coal was expected to be railed from an average of 23 miles distant, presumably from East Somerset pits.[2]

In August, the Company met in Devizes Town Hall and after considering Brunel's plans, resolved that the station in Devizes should be next to the Market Place and as near to the Bear Hotel as reasonably practicable. In September, the Directors offered £100 to the promoters of the 1836 Devizes & Melksham scheme to make use of the original plans and survey documents. In November 1845, some four months after the Wilts, Somerset and Weymouth Railway Act had been passed, Meek wrote to the WSWR, and to the GWR (who were to work the nominally independent system) urging that the junction of the Devizes branch be altered to provide a shorter route to Bradford and Bath. The Directors agreed to prepare a

11

Supplementary Bill altering the junction to Holt, between Staverton and Melksham.

Meanwhile a fresh attempt to put Devizes on a direct line to London had come from the K&A Canal proprietors who, seeing their traffic eroded by the GWR main line opened in 1841, at first contemplated conversion of the canal to a railway but were recommended in August 1845 to build a line alongside the waterway.[3] The canal promoters launched a 'London, Newbury and Bath Direct Railway' scheme following a route via Pewsey Vale. So many schemes for east-west railways were being floated that on 10 October the Mayor of Devizes convened a public meeting to consider this and other routes involving the town. The meeting resolved to support three schemes - including the LN&BDR - of the nine represented. Also discussed was the GWR's proposed extension from Hungerford to Westbury which avoided Devizes on a route to its south.

Snuff manufacturer Paul Anstie declared that:

From the circumstance of Devizes being the central county and Assizes town, with the principal market in . . . Wilts, it is of vital importance that any railway from Hungerford to Westbury and westwards, should pass through Devizes.

The Borough Council pursued this theme with the GWR after the 1846 WSWR Act (to alter the branch junction) had become law; and the LN&BDR Bill, whose promoters opposed the WSWR alterations, defeated. In a memorial to the GWR Directors in September 1846 councillors claimed that Devizes used to enjoy a great deal of east-west through traffic but its trade had been injured by the London-Bristol railway being built via Swindon. They emphasised that Devizes, having 'a very large weekly corn market' and the largest prison in Wiltshire was entitled by its size and position to 'full and efficient railway accommodation'.

The Great Western's tactful reply appears to have reassured the Corporation. Secretary C. A. Saunders said the GWR's intention was to provide the best possible routes from Devizes to Bath and from Hungerford to Exeter:

The Directors are satisfied that these two purposes will be most certainly accomplished by uniting the new line from Hungerford with the Wilts & Somerset line at Devizes . . . while the Exeter line would diverge towards Westbury from a point to the south-east of Devizes to provide the best and shortest route to Plymouth and Falmouth from the Great Western line.

The letter expressed the Directors' promise to consider any suggestions 'leading to the local benefit of Devizes as far as they could'. Alderman Henry Butcher said it conveyed 'a distinct promise . . . of a direct communication from Devizes to London'.[4]

The GWR argued that the proposed new junction at Holt, (facing Bath) and the Bradford-Bathampton line, both now authorised, would create an excellent Devizes-Bath route. However, progress was slow, partly because of difficulty in purchasing land at the Devizes end of the branch, notably with Dr Robert Brabant, who had opposed the original WSWR Bill in 1845, as he lived near the route.

In January 1847, the Directors appointed Henry Cotterell of Bath as Land Surveyor to settle purchases and compensation along the branch. But in April he encountered difficulty over purchase of Devizes Castle estates and houses adjacent to the Bear Hotel, although he reached agreement with the Duke of Somerset in

May over land at Seend. The question of Castle estates was referred to Brunel, presumably to investigate a deviation. Paul Anstie wrote to the Directors in September suggesting alteration of the line at Devizes station site to a lower level, and diversion of the Hungerford extension into Devizes; they replied that the latter was a matter for the GWR's decision but that altering the works at Devizes itself was difficult in view of the progress already made.

In April 1848, the town's two MPs headed a deputation asking for an assurance that the branch would open at the same time as the Thingley–Westbury main line. The Directors declined to 'bind themselves to any such agreement, bearing in mind the financial position and claims of other districts'. By the time the first section of the WSWR to Westbury opened in September, the WSWR was having financial problems. In July 1849 it still had unresolved land purchases at Rowde and with the Diocese of Salisbury at Devizes. The Company sold out in March 1850 to the GWR.

The cost of a large network in a mainly agricultural area had proved too much for the WSWR. The railway mania had evaporated and the GWR itself could scarcely afford to complete the system. Nevertheless, following a May 1852 meeting held in Chippenham, to protest about uncompleted railways, the *Wiltshire Independent* for 3 June 1852 commented that the GWR (which it called 'this faithless company') was now offering to complete the Devizes branch if the inhabitants provided one-third of the cost.

The Borough Council was evidently unimpressed, for it was now actively opposing the GWR's Bill enabling the Company to complete the WSWR Frome-Weymouth line, and also to take over the K&A Canal. A petition to the Mayor from Councillors Anstie and William Cunnington argued that the GWR should have no further powers conferred on it until it used its existing powers to bring the railway to Devizes. On 15 May, the Corporation appointed a six-man Committee including Anstie, Cunnington and the Mayor, to petition the House of Lords against the Bill.

A month later the delegation had to report on a fruitless mission; they had emphasised the damage to Devizes trade caused by uncompleted railways, but the GWR's influence had been 'sufficient to induce their Lordships to refuse any evidence relating to railways'. They had been forced to confine their objections to the question of the GWR having a monopoly of long distance transport between London and the West if it took over the canal. The Lords refused to amend the Bill.[5]

Undaunted, Devizes and other towns served the GWR with Bills of Mandamus to compel it to complete the WSWR lines. Although only one lawsuit – concerning the Bathampton link – was successful, the GWR now bowed to local opinion. Probably the defeat of its Devon & Dorset Railway Bill, aimed at keeping the LSWR out of Devon, persuaded the GWR to move its aspirations back to Wiltshire and Somerset. By an Act of 31 July 1854, the GWR was empowered to raise an additional one million pounds for completion of the network within three years. On 4 August, Devizes Corporation resolved to keep the town clock at 'Railway Time' (Greenwich Time).

Completion of the branch must have been expensive. Steep gradients were needed to bring the line from the meadows of Holt to Devizes, 400 feet above sea level. Park Dale bridge had to be rebuilt when leaking water from the canal caused an embankment to slip.[6] The original 1845 Act had specified a 'good and substantial bridge' over the K&A Canal at Lower Foxhangers. It had to maintain a

DEVIZES
RAILWAY
The Great Western Directors having decided on

OPENING

The Railway for Traffic on

WEDNESDAY, JULY 1st,

THE MAYOR

(In accordance with the strongly expressed wishes of many of his Brother Townsmen,)
requests the Inhabitants of the Town and Neighbourhood who feel an interest in the matter
to MEET HIM AT

THE TOWN-HALL,

ON

MONDAY THE 29th OF JUNE INSTANT,

AT 3 O'CLOCK IN THE AFTERNOON,

To take into consideration and adopt such steps as may be deemed advisable to

Celebrate the Event.

Devizes, June 27th, 1857.

H. BULL, PRINTER, DEVIZES.

3. Poster advertising the opening
of the Holt–Devizes line.

clear waterway of at least thirty feet under one arch. Building materials were to be
agreed between the railway and canal companies. If the railway company failed to
make repairs within seven days' notice from the K&A Canal proprietors, the latter
were empowered to arrange them at the railway's expense.

Devizes station was built in 1856, with an overall roof, and a platform 120 feet
long, some distance from the Market Place. The engine shed was opened in April
1857, its first occupant was *Dreadnought* of the 'Fury' class.[7] The line itself did not
open for traffic until 1 July; the Mayor had hastily convened a meeting on 29 June
to discuss celebrations. He declared the opening day a general holiday and asked
for shops to be closed.

The first excursion from Devizes ran to Weymouth for what the GWR called 'the
very trifling cost of 4s 0d.' Local records suggest it conveyed 1,000 people in 23
carriages; one would have thought this load might have posed problems on the 1-in-
52 Caen Hill bank on the return journey. The first service train from Devizes
arrived at Holt to the strains of 'Hail the Conquering Hero Comes'.[6]

An engine which did fail coming up Caen Hill was *Tityos* an 0-6-0 of the
'Hercules' class, hauling a passenger train from Trowbridge in July 1858.
'Passengers were not a little alarmed by the sudden stopping of the engine and
carriages near the New Prison.' They reached the station on foot.[8]

REFERENCES

1. C. R. Clinker and E. T. MacDermot, *A History of the Great Western Railway,* Vol 1.
2. Wilts, Somerset & Weymouth Railway minutes, 9.7.1844.
3. K. R. Clew, *The Kennet & Avon Canal,* David & Charles.
4. Devizes Borough Council minutes, 30.9.1846.
5. Ibid, 15.6.1852.
6. 'Holt Junction', a *Holt Magazine* supplement, 1966.
7. *Great Western Railway Engine Sheds,* Oxford Publishing Company.
8. *Devizes & Wilts Gazette,* 22.7.1858.

TWO
The Berks & Hants Extension

Even before it opened, the branch line from Holt was regarded by many Devizes people as a poor second best to being on a direct line to London. On 3 June 1852 the *Wiltshire Independent,* no doubt reflecting local frustration at the lack of progress with any rail scheme for Devizes, had declared:

What Devizes wants, what she is morally if not legally entitled to, is to be placed on a direct and through line from London to Bath and the West - in fact that the Hungerford Extension Line be carried on through Devizes.

The same editorial scorned the proposed branch from Holt (and the GWR's offer to complete it if Devizes paid one-third of the cost), as 'a compromise which ... if accepted will deprive Devizes of any chance of being placed on a through line'. Arguing that the town needed an inlet as well as an outlet, the newspaper said Devizes should be content with nothing less than a direct railway from London to the West. However, when completion of the Holt–Devizes line grew nearer, influential men in east and mid-Wiltshire seized the opportunity to forge a link between the new branch and Hungerford, terminus of the Berks & Hants Railway (another line worked by the GWR). The latter had opened from Reading in 1847.

In May 1855, a Committee had been formed for this purpose with the Marquess of Ailesbury, a notable landowner in the Savernake area, as President. The following year the Committee, which included his brother Lord Ernest Bruce MP, former Devizes MP T. Southeron Estcourt, and William Cunnington, were presented with details of the projected route by their Engineer, Mr Ward at a meeting in Devizes Town Hall.

Ward described a line from the station then under construction, through the castle grounds using low ground to its east, thence via Hillworth, Stert, and Beechingstoke. Running along Pewsey Vale the line would follow the K&A Canal between Crofton and Hungerford, but would avoid Marlborough - as a deviation through that town would add £35,000 to a predicted cost of £280,000 (including land acquisition) for the 24½-mile line. The Mayor of Marlborough, while admitting his preference for a route through his town, magnanimously urged his delegation to support the scheme as proposed; he was evidently happy with the promise of 'a first class station' to be provided for the Marlborough area at Burbage Wharf. Lord Ernest Bruce said the Marquess would support the Pewsey route provided it followed the canal at Burbage and a well-appointed station was built there. The Committee voted unanimously to support Ward's route and elected a provisional Committee to carry the scheme forward. Its members included Lord Ailesbury (Chairman), Estcourt (Vice-Chairman), Devizes solicitor William Tugwell and Lord Ernest Bruce.

Notice of their application for a Parliamentary Bill to authorise construction of the line, to be worked and maintained by the GWR, appeared in *The London*

4. A diesel multiple unit leaves Devizes tunnel en route to Patney in the 1960s. This section opened in 1862. (P. Strong)

Gazette for 10 November 1858 under the title 'Berks & Hants Extension Railway'. Solicitors to the Bill included Alexander Meek of Devizes who had worked for the WSWR promoters. With the support of local MPs and the principal landowner (Lord Ailesbury) along its route, the Bill met little opposition and the Company was incorporated by the Act receiving the Royal Assent on 13 August 1859. Construction began early in 1861.

The new line was actually engineered underneath the castle by a 190-yard tunnel, the foundations of which went twenty or thirty feet below the level of the old moat. Many Roman relics were unearthed during excavations for the tunnel and for Pans Lane cutting. Like the branch from Holt, the BHER opened as a broad gauge, single line. Intermediate stations were provided at Woodborough (seven miles from Devizes), Pewsey, Savernake (just east of Burbage Wharf) and Bedwyn. In January 1862, the Directors turned down requests for a station at Patney, claiming Woodborough to be near enough.

In May 1862, with the line nearing completion, Tugwell reminded his fellow Directors of the delays caused to passengers from Devizes to Bath and Bristol by shunting at Holt and change of trains at Trowbridge. The Company called upon the GWR, who were to provide the trains for the new line under the 1859 Act, to facilitate through traffic between Hungerford, Bath and Bristol 'without any delays'.

The *Trowbridge Advertiser* argued that the new line was of little use unless a

16

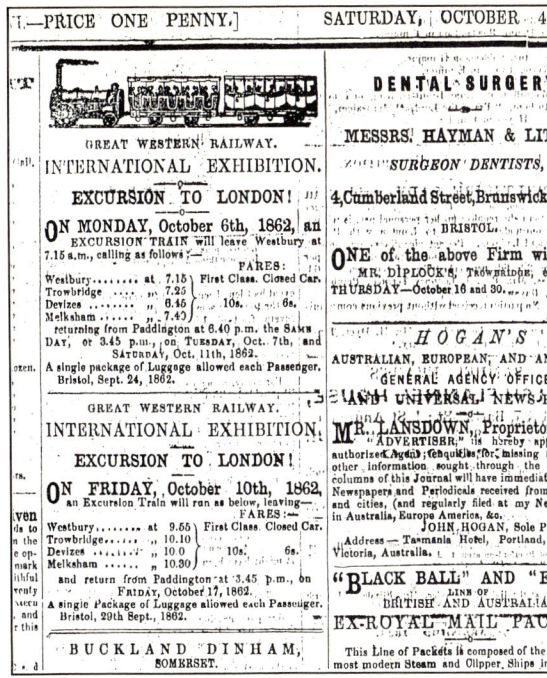
5. Advertisements for excursions to London in the *Trowbridge Advertiser*, shortly before opening of the Devizes–Hungerford line.

northern curve at Bradford Junction, authorised in the original WSWR Act, was built to enable trains to run directly from Devizes to Bath; the article doubted whether people would wish to go to Bath from London or Reading by changing trains at Trowbridge.[1]

A few weeks before the BHER was due to open, Devizes Corporation began advertising the town's new cheese and cattle market in the Reading and Salisbury, as well as local, newspapers. It suggested holding it on the first Thursday of each month, starting on 6 November 1862 if the railway opened that week as promised.[2] The BHER Directors were disappointed with the GWR's proposed timetable, which provided only four trains each way between Hungerford and Devizes; the first down train (8.35 am from Hungerford) had no connection from London while the latest service from Paddington was to be 3.30 pm. The BHER wanted faster trains to allow better connections with London trains at Reading and with Bristol, Salisbury and Weymouth trains at Trowbridge. This was difficult to achieve while there was only one passing loop on the BHE, at Savernake, although loops were provided at Woodborough, Bedwyn and Pewsey in 1863. However, journeys of seventy minutes for passenger trains between Devizes and Hungerford were common in the early years.

In October 1862, just before the new line opened, there were five passenger trains each weekday between Devizes and Trowbridge, taking between twenty-five and forty-five minutes. All except one called at Seend, which had opened to passengers in September 1858. Up trains were allowed fifteen minutes between Seend and Devizes, but only ten minutes vice-versa, presumably because of the incline. Time-

17

tables advertised in the local press showed all up trains calling at Holt Junction but only one down train doing so. The station at Holt was evidently not opened until 1861 and only then as an interchange between the Chippenham–Weymouth line and the Devizes branch, although many villagers had travelled between Holt and Devizes on the day the line opened, according to local records.[3] Seend had been chosen as the site for an intermediate station because of recent iron ore working in the vicinity, but with the extension to Hungerford now imminent, people in the Semington area petitioned the GWR for a station at Outmarsh (where the line already open crossed a turnpike road from Melksham.) Ironically the 200-signature memorial from the clergy and 'principal inhabitants' of the neighbourhood was headed by Walter Long, MP for North Wilts, former Chairman of the WSWR which had turned down the same request in 1847. The petitioners now argued that the GWR's choice of Seend had been misplaced as the ironworks traffic had not 'for some time' lived up to expectations; by contrast a station at Outmarsh would be of great benefit to the Company and to Melksham (two miles distant).[4] Their plea was to be ignored until the next century, however.

Despite the disappointing service offered them by the GWR, the BHE Directors decided to celebrate in style. A special train was arranged to leave Hungerford at 12.00 noon on 4 November 1862 (a week before the line opened for public traffic) and reach Devizes at 1.30 pm for a lavish luncheon in the Corn Exchange. Tickets for the return trip were offered to shareholders for 4s 0d inclusive of luncheon. Several hundred people wined and dined. The train returned from Devizes at 5.00 pm.

Soon after the new line was open to traffic, the GWR's Operating Superintendent conceded some timetable changes but the BHE complained that the GWR charged 'exceedingly high' goods rates for through traffic which 'in many cases prohibited the use of the line'.[5] At its meeting on 21 November, the BHER Board considered that a Sunday service of two trains each way would be desirable, although a Sunday service introduced when the Holt–Devizes line opened had been soon withdrawn when traffic did not match expectations. From December 1862, it appears that a goods train began leaving Hungerford at 8.15 am, and after shunting at stations, was due Devizes at 11.00 am; its return trip left Devizes about 3.30 pm.[6] The Directors proposed to the GWR that passenger carriages be attached to goods trains on Devizes cheese market days, but in January 1864 the GWR said this was not a normal practice on their system and asked whether the BHER would take responsibility for any safety complications. The latter Company replied that a gap between 12.45 pm and 5.45 pm in the up passenger service from Devizes was too great; in any case, mixed trains already operated between Devizes and Trowbridge. In May 1864 the mixed market day train was conceded.

Meanwhile the BHER had engaged James Forbes of the London, Chatham & Dover Railway (and a former GWR Goods Manager), as technical adviser for its now regular meetings with the GWR Management over timetable alterations. Forbes probably carried some weight with his former superior, the GWR's Secretary, Charles Saunders. In its Report for the second half of 1863 the Company announced a 13 percent increase in receipts, due at least in part to improved train services; but as the BHER Directors freely admitted, train services were still far from perfect. An article in the *GWR Magazine* for January 1913 quoted James Drew, the first Bedwyn Station Master, as saying that BHE trains of 1863 had 'coaches open from end to end . . . with seats of bare board'. In December 1870, the Directors complained about the dirtiness of carriages used on their line; the GWR replied that the state of old broad gauge stock was due to 'Board of Trade uncertainties' over conversion of its system to standard gauge.[7]

A frequent grievance was that, despite the sympathetic utterances of senior GWR officers, the latter Company was not doing enough to promote the BHE as a route for through traffic. In September 1866 the BHER complained that Weymouth line passengers bound for Reading and London were not being advised of the Devizes route to the capital. Two months later James Grierson of the GWR promised that 'a large board directing passengers to change at Trowbridge for Paddington via B&HR shall at once be erected'.

He also placated the BHER in December 1870 by issuing an instruction that tickets from Devizes to stations north of Didcot were to be issued at identical fares for travel either via Reading or via Holt and Chippenham; the BHER had complained that much lower rates were being quoted for journeys via the latter (wholly GWR-owned) route. Grierson's assurances did not prevent a similar allegation in July 1871 that Devizes passengers were being 'practically prohibited' from booking to Wolverhampton and beyond via Reading. Similarly, a Berkshire resident complained in April 1871 that the GWR clerk at Cardiff had refused to book him to Hungerford via Devizes, but instead offered him a fare via Didcot and Reading.

Grierson promised to visit the BHE line (again), discuss questions with BHER Secretary Charles Hart (based in an office in Devizes) and enquire into the traffic between South Wales stations and Hungerford. Possibly complaints over routing of journeys arose because clerks at busy stations became accustomed to booking people via the normally most expeditious route. To their credit the GWR agreed that same year to route Weymouth–Paddington excursions via Devizes on a trial basis; response to the first train routed this way on 12 August 1871 was good enough to persuade the parent company to repeat the exercise every third Saturday. The Great Western had also shown a willingness to compromise on timetable matters.

In January 1867, after the BHER had complained that terminating the 8.05 pm train from Trowbridge at Devizes would cripple its westbound traffic, Sir Daniel Gooch had agreed to Hart's request to extend the train to Marlborough (the terminus of a branch opened from Savernake in 1864); but the train was curtailed again by June, when the BHER again pleaded for better westward connections. However, Grierson soon afterwards rescinded a fares increase on the line which Hart claimed had been imposed illegally without his Company being consulted. By October 1867 the BHER was carrying regular Post Office mail traffic.

A venture of the Company which did not materialise was the planned extension from Stert (west of Woodborough) to Westbury, the new route to the South West which the GWR had contemplated in 1845. The BHER had obtained powers to build this line by an Act of 28 June 1866, but disappointing financial results in the next two years, blamed partly on the national recession and partly on unsatisfactory train services, caused the Company to apply to the Board of Trade for a Warrant to abandon the project. This had been granted by early 1870. Had the new line been built then it is possible that Devizes, which it bypassed, would not have enjoyed the substantial train service improvements it gained later in the century.

Nevertheless, the BHE was far from being a failure. By June 1865 it was operating two Sunday trains each way; including a morning Reading-Trowbridge train reaching Devizes at 12.40 pm and an evening train from Reading terminating at Devizes at 8.25 pm.

The first up train on Sundays started from Devizes at 8.30 am. Although it reached Reading in just over two hours, Sunday trains into Paddington were so few and slow that one did not reach the capital by this service until 3.15 pm, having waited at Reading for over three hours! The early evening up train came from Trowbridge (as did the morning train in later years when Devizes engine shed closed), leaving Devizes at 5.25 pm and bringing one to London, via Reading, at 9.40 pm.

The earliest weekday service for London in summer 1865 left Devizes at 7.30 am, calling at all stations to Reading. Five minutes previously, a local train left for Trowbridge, connecting there with a Salisbury-Bristol train reaching the latter city at 9.35 am. It appears that the train service required several engines to be shedded at Devizes, as is suggested by a derailment reported in the *Trowbridge Advertiser* for 29 November 1862: '*Nemesis,* a freight engine of the "Caliph" class, struck a point while shunting in the late morning, blocking the engine house containing two other engines'.

Undoubtedly the BHE's greatest achievement was to bring Devizes much closer to London in terms of journey times. A day trip to the capital had just about been possible in pre-BHE days via Holt and Chippenham when special connecting trains were provided (e.g. for an International Exhibition on 6 October 1862, first class return fare 10s 0d), but excursionists normally returned on a later day. By using the 8.22 am weekday train from Trowbridge (8.50 am from Devizes) in 1865, one reached Paddington at 11.15 am. The latest return service from London was 6.15 pm (BHER minutes suggest that, for a time, the GWR was persuaded to run the latter train through to Bristol with reversal at Trowbridge).[8]

Most of the tourist excursion fares from Devizes at this time either involved travel via Trowbridge (for West Country resorts) or via Holt to Northern or Scottish destinations, but people holidaying on the South or East Coasts could normally travel via the BHE and London. So useful did people find this link for through travel that in June 1872 the BHER persuaded the GWR to attach the first up train to a London train at Reading, to enable passengers for the North to reach Paddington in time to catch the 12.00 noon train from King's Cross.

Freight traffic grew on the BHE despite the national economic situation. By 1870 a goods train was leaving Reading at 6.20 am, shunting at most stations between Newbury and Devizes, where it remained from 10.25 am till 11.15 am. After crossing the 10.00 am mixed train from Trowbridge it proceeded to Seend and normally terminated at Holt, though it ran to Trowbridge if required. A return goods train for Reading left Holt at 12.40 pm, lingering at Devizes from 1.10 pm to 2.00 pm. There were also 9.10 am and 3.50 pm mixed trains from Devizes to Trowbridge in the 1870 timetable, plus a 7.40 am goods Trowbridge-Devizes.

REFERENCES

1. *Trowbridge Advertiser*, 25.10.1862. ,
2. Devizes Borough Council minutes, 13.10.1862.
3. H. I. Quayle, 'Open or Shut?', *Railway Magazine*, March 1981.
4. *Trowbridge Advertiser*, 1.11.1862.
5. Berks & Hants Extension Railway minutes of Directors' Meetings, 19.12.1862.
6. Ibid, 21.11.1862.
7. Ibid, 16.12.1870.
8. Ibid, 20.5.1864.

THREE
An Age of Improvement

Devizes Corporation were still looking for better things from the BHE when, in June 1872, they expressed the hope that extra railway facilities would result if the Secretary of State for War accepted the suggestion that a central depot for the Wilts and Dorset militia be sited near the town.[1] War Secretary Cardwell rejected the proposal on health grounds; he claimed that 'a prevalence of fever' linked with the local water supply made a Devizes site unsuitable. Later that year, traders in Newbury and Hungerford complained to the GWR that the broad gauge of the Reading–Holt line was responsible for delays to traffic originating on the other companies' lines. In the event, conversion to standard gauge took place over the weekend of 27 June 1874. Timings of Devizes–Trowbridge trains had been adjusted during conversion of the WSWR main line through Holt a week or so earlier; no trains ran from Devizes to Trowbridge on Sunday 21 June.

Inspecting the converted lines in September, the GWR General Manager, James Grierson recommended the removal of Devizes engine shed to Trowbridge, saying it occupied space 'much required for traffic purposes'. The growth of Devizes in population and as a market centre was generating more freight business. Grierson was accompanied by Captain Tyler from the Board of Trade; they agreed that work on building a water tank near to the loco shed should cease. It was resolved to build it 'where it is not likely to interfere with any of the sidings or the future arrangements of the station'.[2] Hence the siting of the tank on the hillside above the goods yard.

The same inspection party recommended improvements to the office on the platform at Holt, which had become a fully-fledged station with booking facilities on 1 April; But not until November 1877, following representations to the GWR by villagers, did it gain road access.[3] In July 1877, the Board of Trade had to remind the GWR that 'certain matters were unsatisfactory' following Colonel Yolland's inspection of new works between Reading and Holt; work outstanding included the provision of shelter on Devizes down platform, which they understood was in hand. A more serious complaint concerned the lack of gradient boards on these and other GWR-operated lines; the Board of Trade's view that train crews should have a proper knowledge of the route's gradients was appropriate in view of the inclines between Holt and Devizes. In its letter, dated 18 July, the Board of Trade said that, in the absence of an assurance from the GWR to comply, it was considering laying the Inspector's report before Parliament; an extreme option it did not expect to take would be to close the line.[9]

In June 1881 the GWR agreed to put on two extra trains each weekday between Devizes and Trowbridge in response to a petition. Local politicians thought they would have a stronger hand after the BHER sold out to the GWR on 1 July 1882.

The town's MP, Sir Thomas Bateson, made good use of his friendship with Sir

Daniel Gooch to arrange for a deputation to meet the Directors. Sir Thomas headed a public meeting in the Town Hall in March 1883, called to discuss 'the probable effect on Devizes and neighbourhood of proposed railway schemes'. The proposed scheme in most people's minds was the GWR's plan for a Stert to Westbury route as part of a new main line to the South West. The discussion centred on the short-comings of existing train services. Bateson read a sympathetic letter from Gooch admitting that services on the Berks & Hants fell below local expectations, but that the GWR had only just taken over the line and that timings on the single track route were geared as far as possible to connections at Reading and Trowbridge – 'a most difficult object to accomplish'.[4]

Speaker after speaker slated slow, infrequent services from Devizes, with poor connections at Trowbridge. Alderman Stephen Reynolds claimed there was 'no place worse served than Devizes'; H. E. Medlicott, quoting instances of long waits at Trowbridge for trains to Bath (e.g. seventy minutes' wait from the 6.45 pm ex-Devizes) or Salisbury, said that the junction town was profiting through the money people spent there while waiting for trains. Condemning 'exceedingly bad' journey times going west from Devizes, he carried a resolution for a good interchange station between the Devizes line and the planned Stert–Westbury line. Medlicott argued that the town had such a bad service that meeting a friend at 6.00 pm at the far corner of the County necessitated leaving Devizes at 10.00 am!

A more constructive resolution moved by Charles Colston of Roundway Park that the 'tedious and most unsatisfactory' service westwards from Devizes be replaced with through trains from Reading to Bath and Bristol was also passed..All these points were put to the GWR Board by a deputation including Bateson, Mr Sotheron Estcourt MP, the Town Clerk and Borough Council members John Marsh and George Mead on 5 April. The Corporation stressed the poor service to London; except by the 8.01 am train, (7.30 am ex-Trowbridge). Paddington could not be reached until 3.53 pm. Moreover there was nearly a five-hour gap between the first and second services to London from Devizes. As the final service eastwards (8.05 pm ex-Trowbridge) did not reach London until 11.25 pm, the delegation claimed Devizes had only two trains to the capital suitable for 'family or general travellers'. They also instanced journey times of two to two-and-three-quarter hours from Devizes to Salisbury, and one-and-a-half hours to Chippenham, and cited the postponement of business at the last Quarter-Sessions in Devizes until after 1.00 pm because magistrates from Swindon, Salisbury and Malmesbury could not reach Devizes before then without leaving around seven in the morning. Gooch responded to these criticisms by promising a review of the timetable and reiterated the Board's intention to double the BHR from Hungerford to Westbury and provide a transfer station at Stert when the new line was built.

An improved service to London soon materialised. From July the gap in morning trains to Reading was filled by a 9.45 am train from Trowbridge, departing Devizes at 10.14 am and giving a Paddington arrival of 1.50 pm; this service replaced the 9.00 am Trowbridge–Devizes train. In the down direction, a 2.10 pm Reading–Trowbridge train, off Devizes at 4.20 pm, replaced the 4.50 pm Devizes–Trowbridge. By running the Sunday morning up train 1¾ hours earlier, London could be reached at 10.25 am instead of 3.15 pm; one now had to leave Devizes at 6.32 am instead of 8.17 am but waiting time at Reading was cut from over three hours to

Table No. 33. For Intermediate Stations between London and Reading, see pages 18 to 25.

FARES From PADDINGTON (By Ordinary Train.)		DOWN TRAINS.	Clss.	WEEK DAYS.												SUNDAYS	
Single.	Return.							B			B	B			B		

Table body contains dense numerical timetable data (down trains): London (Paddington), Windsor, Reading, Aldermaston, Midgham, Thatcham, Newbury, Kintbury, Hungerford, Bedwyn, Savernake, Marlborough, Pewsey, Woodborough, Devizes, Seend, Holt, Trowbridge, Bradford, Freshford, Limpley Stoke, Bathampton, Bath, Bristol, Trowbridge (for Salisbury), Salisbury, Trowbridge (for Weymouth), Yeovil (Pen Mill), Dorchester, Weymouth.

Fares to Reading		UP TRAINS.	Class	WEEK DAYS.											Sundays	
Single.	Return.															

Up trains: Weymouth (for Trowbridge), Dorchester, Yeovil (Pen Mill), Trowbridge, Salisbury (for Trowbridge), Bristol, Bath, Bathampton, Limpley Stoke, Freshford, Bradford, Trowbridge, Holt Junction, Seend, Devizes, Woodborough, Pewsey, Marlborough, Savernake, Bedwyn, Hungerford, Kintbury, Newbury, Thatcham, Midgham, Aldermaston, Theale, Reading, Windsor, London (Paddington Stn).

B Salisbury and Weymouth Passengers to and from Devizes and Hungerford Line change Carriages at Holt or Trowbridge.
B Horses and Carriages are not conveyed by these Trains as between London and Reading.
C Horses and Carriages are only conveyed by this Train between Trowbridge and Newbury.
A Passengers for Windsor do not in all cases leave Reading by the same Trains as the London Passengers. Enquiry at Reading should be made.

TABLE No. 35a. ## WEYMOUTH AND PORTLAND RAILWAY.
All Trains are First, Second, and Third. For Main Line Trains to and from Weymouth, see pages 42 and 43.

FARES.		DOWN TRAINS.	WEEK DAYS.	SUNDAYS.
Single.	Return.			

Down trains: Weymouth, Rodwell, Portland.

FARES.		UP TRAINS.	WEEK DAYS.	SUNDAYS.
Single.	Return.			

Up trains: Portland, Rodwell, Weymouth.

6. Passenger timetable for July 1883.

24

fifteen minutes. Meanwhile the GWR opposed the Bristol and London & South Western Railway Bill, designed to provide a competitive route via Amesbury and Bratton. Farmers around Tilshead supported the proposal, claiming they needed a nearer railhead than Devizes for sending produce and receiving coal, but the GWR claimed Salisbury Plain was adequately served by their lines through Devizes and Warminster; if a third line was built in a sparsely populated district all three would be struggling.[5] In the event the B&LSWR never materialised; its route bypassed Bradford and Trowbridge whose Town Commissioners hoped for an upgraded route to London via Devizes instead.

Freight traffic continued to increase. Coal from the Radstock area was being railed to Devizes for the town's gasworks by 1889, when a contract was signed with local merchant Messrs J. F. & J. W. Phipp to deliver 2,700 tons of best quality gas coal from the station in the year ending 31 March 1890.

In October, Devizes Urban Sanitary Authority engaged Messrs H. J. & W. E. Sainsbury, who operated a railway goods and parcel agency in Northgate Street, to deliver approximately 1,500 tons in six months. A condition of the new contract was that if the coal became wet, through exposure to the weather, the Authority could at once determine the contract. Messrs Phipp regained the contract for most of 1891, being required to order trucks from Huish Colliery Radstock, carriage paid to Devizes station, 'properly covered so that the coal shall always be dry'.

By June 1889, an iron latticework footbridge had been provided between the two platforms at Devizes. The *Wiltshire Times* for 8 June commented 'such a structure has long been agitated for ... owing to the great danger of crossing the line with

7. Devizes station showing overall roof, probably about the turn of the century. Note the smoke stacks on the train shed chimneys and the horse and carriage. (Lens of Sutton)

8. The Fish Bridge, scene of the June 1889 shooting incident. The bridge is in its final rebuilt form and this photograph was taken shortly before its demolition in 1969. (P. Strong)

much shunting'. At the same time waiting accommodation on the down platform was improved.

The same week, the line was the scene of a bizarre crime of passion. Emily Lister, aged twenty-nine, newly-appointed Headmistress of Devizes British School, had been followed to the town by her former admirer, Gus Keeling. On Friday 7 June, the couple were seen quarrelling at the station. Just before the 11.10 am Reading-Trowbridge train was due, Miss Lister bought a ticket to Bristol. At the last minute Keeling bought a ticket to Seend. They boarded an empty, third class compartment but, according to the Guard, were looking in opposite directions. Passengers in adjoining compartments later admitted hearing 'loud quarrelling'.

As the train ran over the Fish Bridge, Keeling fired two shots, the girl fell out of the window and rolled down the embankment. A Mr Brice travelling on the train saw Keeling aiming a revolver at Lister; he got out of his own compartment onto the footboard of the carriage to try and contact the Guard, as the carriage had no communication cord. Seeing Brice on the footboard, GWR Inspector Upchurch from Reading stopped the train in 200–300 yards near Seend brickyard gate. Meanwhile Miss Lister had been found, bleeding heavily, by a platelayer named Burgess; who with George Williams got Miss Lister transported to Devizes Cottage Hospital, in a conveyance lent by a Mr Wheeler living near the scene.

Miss Lister lost an eye though she eventually recovered and returned to teaching. Keeling had been less fortunate. His mutilated body was found beside the track; Upchurch told the inquest that the dead man probably intended to escape from the

26

train along the footboard, but the train was moving too fast and he fell under it. Two letters from Lister were found on Keeling, one an affectionate note from an address in Brighton (where both were previously teachers). The second letter, written from Devizes, was a cold and distant goodbye. It transpired that Keeling had wanted to marry her, but she had turned against him on discovering he had spent some time in an asylum. Almost penniless, Keeling had boarded the train to ask her for money and had shot her when she refused. His family seems to have disowned him, for he had a pauper's funeral attended only by a press reporter.

A much happier railway event that summer was the running of two excursion trains on Friday 26 July; when the annual outings of Alderman Mead the grocer and Devizes' Workmen's Club took nearly 1,000 people to Portsmouth, where cheap trips were organised around the Naval Dockyard and to the Isle of Wight. Leaving Devizes around 5.30 am, the trains were due at Portsmouth around 9.00 am in order to see Queen Victoria arrive in the Royal yacht. Royalty also attracted excursion trains to Devizes. In May 1893, 6,000 people came by rail to see the Centenary of the Royal Wilts Yeomanry, visited by the Prince of Wales. The train service eastwards had been increased to six weekday departures from Devizes, although the 7.36 am train (7.00 am from Trowbridge) was of little value as a Reading or London service (except to third class 'Parliamentary' ticket holders) because it was overtaken by the 7.36 am ex-Trowbridge which called only at Devizes (8.00 am), Savernake, Hungerford and Newbury before Reading.

Traders and councillors in Devizes still expected further improvements. Alderman Mead presided at a meeting on 5 March 1895 calling for Devizes slip coaches to be provided from Weymouth expresses routed via the planned Stert–Westbury line; doubling of track from Hungerford to Holt; better connctions at Trowbridge for Bath and Bristol; and more sidings at Devizes.

Need for the latter was argued by Alderman Brown who said coal sometimes took thirty days to get from Radstock owing to lack of siding space; a Mr Barnett cited a consignment of sheep dying in a delayed transit to the town, and said two trucks of hurdles from Bedwyn had to be over-carried to Holt and doubled back two days later owing to insufficient room in Devizes goods yard.

The meeting had also suggested utilising the newly-built northern curve at Bradford Junction to permit direct running from Devizes to Bristol without reversal at Trowbridge. Frost damage in the unlined parts of Box Tunnel in February had persuaded the GWR to hastily lay the new spur, opened on 11 March, to avoid the reversal of Paddington–Bristol trains at Trowbridge after their diversion through Melksham. From October a through Bristol–Devizes–Paddington express started using the new curve. It started from Exeter at 8.25 am as a semi-fast, left Bristol at 11.36 am calling only at Bath, Devizes (dep. 12.33 pm) and Newbury to reach the capital at 2.35 pm. In January 1899 the maximum load of this train up Caen Hill bank was 64 wheels of eight-wheeled stock, and 68 wheels of mixed stock; an assisting engine was to be provided from Bristol if necessary.[6] The train continued to run until 1958, leaving Bristol variously between 11.00 am and noon, though it was to terminate at Reading after 1939.

By January 1896 there were six trains each way on weekdays between Trowbridge and Reading plus a 2.30 pm Devizes–Hungerford service on Thursdays only. From May the first up train (6.45 am from Trowbridge, 7.21 am off Devizes),

TROWBRIDGE to PADDINGTON via DEVIZES.

	7 58	9 48	11 47	12 49	3 9	3 57 5 30	0 47	8 32	3 07 42
Chippenham	7 58	9 48	11 47	12 49	3 9	3 57 5 30	0 47	8 32	3 07 42
Dauntsey		10 6	12 24		3 25	5 53			3 12 8 3
Wootton Bassett		10 18	12 36		3 37	6 6			3 22 8 14
Swindon	8 40	10 28	12 50	1 15	3 48	4 36 6 18	7 15	9 25	3 30
Swindon d	9 2	10 53	1 7	1 25	3 57	4 45 6 58	7 25	9 37	6 35
Paddington a	1032	12 33	2 40	3 5	5 4C	6 15 8 30	9 10	11'5	

TROWBRIDGE to PADDINGTON via DEVIZES.	a.m	a.m	a.m	a.m	a.m		p.m	p.m	p.m	p.m	p.m	a.m	p.m
Trowbridge	6 45	7 15		9 35	11 43	1238		3 40	5 55	5 25	
Holt	6 56			9 45	11 52			3 50	6 52	9 7	6	4 5	5 34
Seend	7 5			9 53	12 0	1253		3 58	7	0 9	15	6 13	5 43
Devizes	7 21	7 39		10 10	12 10	1238	1	8 2*30	4 18	7 17	9 25	6 23	5 53
Woodboro'	7 39			10 25			1 24	2 44	4 33	7 33		6 45	6 15
Pewsey	7 46	7 59	8	13	10 34		1 34	2 52	4 42	7 43		6 58	6 25
Marlboro' .d		7 52	7 52	10 25		1240	1 30	2 35	4 17	7 37	
Marlboro'a	8 35		11 5		1 21	2 15	3 20	5 15	8 15	
Savernake	8 11	8 3C	10 47		1 51	4 83	3 4	5 5	7 56		7 10	6 38
Bedwyn		8 39	10 56		1 57	3 11	5	3 8	5	p.m	7 20	6 49
Hungerford	8 27	8 53	11 8		2 9	3 20	5	15	8 18	9 48	7 31	7 1
Kintbury		9 0	11 15		2 16		5 28	25	9 48	7 38	7 8
Newbury	8 42	9 15	11 30		1 37	2 30	5	36	8 40	10 0	7 52	7 25
Reading a	9 9	16	1 12	19		3 11	6	19	9 20	1030	8 35	8 10
Paddington		1010	1055	1 40		2 45	4 22	7	35	11 5	1145	1020	9 20

PADDINGTON to TROWBRIDGE via DEVIZES.

	a.m	a.m	a.m	a.m	a.m	p.m	p.m	p.m	p.m	p.m	a.m	a.m	p.m
Paddington		6 30	9 2c	9 55		1 50	4	0 5	15	7 15		9 20	4 55
Reading		7 55	10 15	11 25		3	5	4 55	6 10	8 15		10 35	6 30
Newbury		8 46	10 59	12 18		3 52	5 43	6 38	9 5		11 21	7 18
Kintbury		8 57	11 10	12 29		4	5 54	9 16		11 32	7 29
Hungerford		9 6	11 16	12 40		4 13	6	3 6	53	9 27		11 41	7 38
Bedwyn		9 16		12 50		4 24	6 14		9 37		11 51	7 48
Savernake		9 27		1 2		4 37	6 25	7	10'9	47		12 1	7 58
Marlboro' .d		9 3		12 40		4 17	6	0 6	52		
Marlboro'a		9 48		1 21		5 15	6 42	7 27		
Pewsey		9 38		1 13		4 49	6 37	7 21	9 57		12 12	8 9
Woodboro'		9 47	a.m	1 23		4 58	6 47		10 5		12 22	8 19
Devizes	6 30	8 35	10 6	11 0	1 38	2 25	5 16	7	0 7	45	1021	8 35	10 40	8 35
Seend	6 38	8 43	1014	11 8	1 46	2 33	5 24		1029	8 43	12 50	8 43
Holt	6 46	8 51	1022	11 16	1 54	2 42	5 32		1037	8 51	12 59	8 51
Trowbridge	6 54	8 57	1028	11 24	2 0	2 49	5 38	8 57	1 5	8 57

A train leaves Devizes weekdays at 7.57 p.m., Seend 8.7, arr. at Holt 8.15.

SWINDON to HIGHWORTH.

	a.m	a.m	a.m	p.m	p.m	p.m	p.m	p.m
Swindon	7 0 9	5 11 15	1 45	4 35 5	45 7 50
Stratton	7 7 9 14	11 22	1 53	4 46 5	55 7 58
Stanton	7 19 9 22	11 33	2 1 4 55	6	4 8 6
Hannington	7 35 9 28	11 43	2 7 5	2'6 14	8 12
Highw'rth	7 50 9 36	11 55	2 15 5	10 6	23 8 20

Sundays—Swindon 3.45, Stratton 3.55, Stanton 4.4, Hannington 4.11, Highworth 4.23

HIGHWORTH to SWINDON.

	a.m	a.m	a.m	p.m	pm	pm	p.m	p.m
Highw'h	5 20	8 10	9 50	1215	3	0	5260	6 41
Hannn'gtn	5 26	8 18	9 56	1221	3	7	5266	41 8 41
Stanton	5 32	8 24	10 3	1227	315	532	6 49	8 60
Stratton	5 42	8 32	1012	1235	325	540	7	0'9 5
Swindon	5 42	8 40	1020	1245	340	548	7	10'9 25

Sundays—Highworth 7.0, Hannington 7.8, Stanton 7.16, Stratton 7.28, Swindon 7.33.

MALMESBURY to DAUNTSEY.

	a.m	a.m	a.m	p.m	p.m	p.m	p.m
Malm'sbry	7 15	9 10	1050	1 15	2 55	4	50 6 5C
Somerford	7 27	9 22	11 2	1 32	3 7	5	7'7 5
Dauntsey	7 35	9 30	1110	1 40	3 15	5	15'7 13

Sundays—Malmesbury 5.40, Somerford 5.55, Dauntsey 6.3.

DAUNTSEY to MALMESBURY.

	a.m	a.m	p.m	p.m	p.m	p.m	p.m
Dauntsey	8 17	10 15	1145	2 25	4 0	6	08 25
Somerford	8 28	10 23	1158	2 33	5 56	8 8 33
Malm'sbry	8 40	10 35	1210	2 45	4 10	6	20 8 45

Sundays—Dauntsey 7.20, Somerford 7.28 Malmesbury 7.40.

BRISTOL to TROWBRIDGE, SALISBURY & PORTSMOUTH.

	a.m	a.m	a.m	p.m	p.m	p.m	p.m	p.m	p.m	p.m			p.m	p.m	p.m
Bristol	6 5	8 12	1C 0	11 0	11;23	1230	1 33	2 15	3 55 5	0 5;30			6 06	42	8 40
Bath	6 23	8 36	10 21	1130	11 43	1255	2 62	37,4	12 5	15 7	50		6 32	7	9	10 11
Bathampton	6 34	8 46	10 31		2 49	5 27			6 44	7 20	9 20
Lply. Stoke	6 43	8 55	10 40		1 9	2 21	2 58	4	30 5 36			6 53	7 29	9 29
Freshford	6 47	8 59	10 44		1 13	2 25	3	5 40			6 58	7 34
Bradford	6 53	9 6	10 51		1 42	2 32	3	12 5 48			7 3	7 40
Trowbridge	7 8	9 18	11 3		12 12	1 36	2 40	3	23 4 48	6	6 18	6 28	7 16	7 50	9 48
Westbury	d 7 18	9 26	11 11		1 44	3 32	6 14		6 36		8 16	9 56
Westbury	d 7 30	9 29	11 15		1 45	3 38		6 39			9 59

9. Passenger timetable for July 1900 as printed in *The Wiltshire Times*.

now terminated at Savernake where it seems to have been shunted clear of the 7.20 am Trowbridge (7.46 am Devizes) express before forming an all-stations train to Reading. The fast train enabled one to reach Paddington at 10.10 am. A later down train was provided: one could now leave London at 7.00 pm and Reading at 8.05 pm to reach Devizes the same night, compared with latest departure times of 5.15 pm and 6.09 pm in January 1892. Extra Devizes–Trowbridge trains were now operating, including an 8.35 am from Devizes and 11.43 am from Trowbridge. However, the last up train, leaving Trowbridge at 8.38 pm now went no further than Devizes, the previous train (6.38 pm Trowbridge) continuing to Reading instead. Persuading the GWR to run the 8.35 am Devizes–Trowbridge on Mondays, as well as other weekdays, had been another achievement of Alderman Mead and his campaigners, who rather contradicted the claim by G. A. Sekon in his *History of the Great Western Railway,* published in 1895, that none of the towns on the Berks & Hants route were 'of much importance'. In the official Guide to the GWR for 1893, Devizes station is listed as having a bookstall; and providing foot-warmers to passengers in the winter, the nearest other stations with this luxury were Trowbridge, Marlborough, Hungerford and Chippenham.

An interesting feature of the 1880s and 1890s was the annual supper for Devizes station staff. On a Friday evening in January 1883, twenty-one sat down to dinner in the Royal Oak Inn. 'The usual loyal, patriotic and complimentary toasts were drunk with great enthusiasm'. Station Master Thomas Abrahams and six others

28

sang 'several capital songs'. The party finished at 2.00 am.[7] The 1895 party for station staff, held in the Bear Hotel, toasted their surgeon Dr Murray Gray who was shortly to begin giving them First Aid classes; also toasted was the Station Master, Mr Neville, as 'the most popular Station Master on the line'.[8] Two weeks later the Permanent Way staff were treated to dinner in the Crown Hotel. Fifty guests included the Mayor (Alderman Mead) and Mr Neville.

REFERENCES

1. Devizes Borough Council minutes.
2. GWR General Manager's report – 'Alteration of gauge of lines, Wilts, Somerset & Weymouth line and branches'.
3. 'A Last Look at Holt Junction', *Holt Magazine*, 1967.
4. *Wiltshire Times*, 24.3.1883.
5. Ibid, 21.4.1883.
6. *Railway Magazine*, April 1940.
7. *Wiltshire Times*, 27.1.1883.
8. Ibid, 2.2.1895.
9. Public Record Office, Ref. Rail 253/710.

FOUR
A Branch Line Again

Nearly fifty years after it had first proposed a main line to the West via Hungerford and Westbury, the Great Western obtained an Act in 1894 authorising a new double track route from Stert to Westbury and doubling of the BHE from Hungerford to Stert. Construction began in 1897.

The new line opened to passengers on 1 October 1900. A new station, called Patney & Chirton Junction, was provided about a mile east of where the new link forked away from the original line to Devizes, still single track. Intermediate stations were opened on the new line at Lavington and Edington & Bratton.

Devizes was now on a single track branch from Patney to Holt, but Reading-Trowbridge and Paddington-Frome trains continued to use it rather than the new line, which at first had a service of local trains connecting at Patney or Woodborough with trains routed via Devizes. The 5.15 pm Paddington-Frome service, hitherto non-stop from Pewsey to Devizes, began calling at Woodborough where a connecting train to Westbury was provided.

Paddington-Weymouth expresses began running via Lavington in 1901 but Devizes also benefited. The 9.35 am Paddington-Weymouth train now slipped a coach at Patney which was worked into Devizes arriving exactly two hours after departure from London. This service continued until 1910. In July 1902 the 5.00 pm Paddington-Weymouth began to slip a coach at Savernake at 6.35 pm which formed a stopping train to Devizes (arr. 7.18 pm in early 1903) and Trowbridge.

The best two Devizes-London services early in 1903 were the 6.45 am Frome, leaving Devizes at 7.45 am to reach Paddington at 10.10 am; and the 11.40 am Bristol-Paddington express taking just over two hours from Devizes.

Another boost for Devizes came in July 1906 when it gained its fastest service from London so far. This was the 3.00 pm Paddington-Weston-super-Mare which called only at Reading and Newbury before reaching Devizes at 4.51 pm; thereafter it was non-stop to Bath although it would set down passengers at Bradford from Newbury and beyond. In later years the train acquired additional stops. Its London-Devizes running time after the Second World War was fifteen minutes *slower.*

By now the Patney-Westbury line was also used by expresses between London and Devon or Cornwall, as a new section of main line across the Somerset Levels had also opened in July 1906, giving such expresses a shorter route than via Bristol. The Devizes branch did not pass into limbo, however. As well as half-a-dozen trains each way between Reading and Trowbridge (including the direct London services) on weekdays, there were also a few Devizes-Trowbridge services. A market day train from Newbury to Devizes ran in the late morning, returning in the early afternoon.

The public timetable for January-April 1903 advertised a 6.00 am Paddington-

10. Patney station, looking towards the junction, taken in about 1920. Note the milk churns on, and outside the down platform. (Mowat Collection)

Trowbridge service reaching Devizes at 9.19 am and Seend at 9.55 am, conveying horses, carriages and milk cans only. The return workings included a train back on Sunday evenings, overtaken at Devizes by the up passenger train.

It did not reach London until midnight.

Local passenger traffic on the branch was energetically promoted by the intro-duction of Steam Railmotors from 1 October 1906, some three years after the GWR had first employed them on its system.[1] These trains consisted of a locomotive engine enclosed in the centre of a carriage, they offered quicker turnround times because there was no separate loco to run round the train. Built with retractable steps they could pick up and set down passengers almost anywhere, a boon to rural dwellers. Indeed, Semington gained its long-awaited station with the start of the Railmotor service between Trowbridge, Devizes and Patney.

Actually the station at Semington was a 'halt' or very basic platform, not long enough or high enough to accommodate trains of normal length. The success of halts opened at Staverton and Lacock in 1905, served by Railmotors between Trowbridge and Chippenham, had encouraged the GWR to erect halts on the Devizes branch at Semington and, in 1909 at Sells Green (though called Bromham & Rowde Halt). In the May 1909 timetable seven Railmotor services operated each way on weekdays, plus the 8.35 am Devizes-Trowbridge on Sundays. A new late evening service was provided from Trowbridge to Devizes and back by a Rail-motor; in May 1909 it left Devizes at 10.40 pm, seventeen minutes after the 8.18 pm Reading-Trowbridge. Railmotors were providing about half the weekday depar-tures from Devizes, including an afternoon Devizes-Frome service which was altered by 1911 to run from Hungerford to Trowbridge. Conventional trains included the 11.40 am ex-Bristol and 3.00 pm ex-Paddington expresses; also a 9.53 am Reading-Bristol semi-fast.

The GWR at this time offered a variety of excursion fares. Stations within twenty miles or so of Devizes offered Thursday Market Day tickets to the town, to travel out by specified trains although one could normally return on any train the same day. In January 1905 the morning Bristol–Paddington express was carrying Market Ticket passengers from Bradford-on-Avon to Devizes at a third class fare of 1s 7d; six years previously that express had only called at Bradford if there were first class passengers for London. A Market Ticket to Devizes was also offered from Calne for 2s 4d despite a circuitous route via Chippenham and Holt. Devizes and Seend sold Market Tickets to Warminster (Saturdays), Trowbridge (Tuesdays and Saturdays) and Frome (Wednesdays).

Period excursion tickets to London advertised in the summer of 1905, using the 8.55 am service from Trowbridge (9.15 am from Seend, 9.30 am Devizes) on Fridays, stipulated return from London the following Friday or Friday week by the 1.12 pm ex-Paddington, changing at Reading. Third class return fares were 8s 6d from Seend, 8s 0d from Devizes.

Other destinations with weekend fares from Devizes at this time included Weymouth, Bournemouth, Weston-super-Mare and Cheddar; passengers travelled out on Friday or Saturday, returning on the Sunday, Monday or Tuesday. These tickets were available first, second or third class. Similar fares were available in May 1905 from Devizes to Plymouth, Bristol, Leamington and Worcester.[2]

Market Tickets to and from Devizes were still very much in evidence in 1913, when half-day returns were also being marketed to help fill lunchtime and afternoon trains. These were offered on Wednesdays and Saturdays from Devizes and Seend to Bath or Bristol; also on Wednesdays (as in 1905) from Devizes to Pewsey, Savernake or Trowbridge. A 7d half-day ticket from Seend to Devizes on Saturdays in October 1913 allowed passengers the option of alighting at Bromham & Rowde on the return journey.

A late afternoon train took Holt, Seend and Devizes passengers to London on Christmas Eve 1913 at third class return fares of 10s 0d, 9s 0d, and 8s 6d respectively. They were permitted to return from Paddington by an afternoon train on specified days. A Whitsun excursion returning from Paddington to Bristol on 14 May 1913 was advertised to leave the capital at 1.05 am with the note 'this train will stop five minutes at Devizes'. It seems reasonable to assume the note was to warn Bristolians not to alight there in the small hours while the train stopped for water.

By May 1914 the 6.18 am Devizes–Trowbridge train had disappeared. The earliest westbound train on weekdays from Devizes was now the 8.00 am to Trowbridge, which continued to run with minor retimings and changes of destination until the line closed in 1966.

The First World War brought a great increase in rail traffic. Troops bound for the Front marched from Devizes barracks to the station with a Regimental Band. The railway also brought Canadian troops billeted in Devizes along with their provisions. Edgar Cross, later to become Station Master at Patney, has recalled how goods clerks in Devizes received news of the war from colleagues in London, who wrote snippets of information on invoices.[3]

After the war Devizes enjoyed another fast train from the capital. In 1922, the 5.55 pm from Paddington was first stop Newbury and non-stop from Savernake to Devizes, reached at 8.01 pm. (This was about half-an-hour faster to Devizes than the 6.00 pm from Paddington thirty years later which detached a Devizes portion at Newbury.) After Devizes, the 5.55 pm ex-Paddington continued to Trowbridge, calling at Seend and Holt, but the line no longer received slip coaches. These were expensive and relatively dangerous to operate, being restricted in later years to major junctions and traffic centres. Railmotors worked eleven of twenty-one weekday departures from Devizes in October 1922. They were shedded at Trowbridge until that loco depot closed in 1923, when they were transferred to Westbury shed. The pre-war Sunday morning train from Devizes to Trowbridge no longer ran.

Railmotors were phased out in the late 1920s and cut-price tickets tended now to be for long distance rather than local travel. Buses were taking much of the short distance passenger market. Rail was still vastly quicker for travel to London. The daily Greyhound coach introduced in 1926 took $5\frac{3}{4}$ hours from Devizes compared with about $2\frac{1}{4}$ hours by the fastest train.

Auto-trains came to dominate the short distance stopping services on the line in the 1930s. Unlike Railmotors, they had a conventional locomotive attached to one or two carriages but could be driven from the windowed carriage end, thus still avoiding the need for the loco to run round. In October 1935, eight of the twelve weekday services in the up direction were auto-trains, still referred to in timetables as 'Rail Motor Cars'. As auto-trains could reverse easily at locations without run-round facilities, the GWR was able to make Pans Lane Halt, opened in 1929 east of Devizes tunnel, the starting point and terminus of certain local trains. In the mid and late 1930s the 5.52 pm auto-train from Trowbridge terminated at Pans Lane as did the late evening up train.

Just before the Second World War, Devizes had six weekday services to London and back via Newbury; two each way were direct. Average journey times were about $2\frac{1}{2}$ hours. There were also a few connections available via Holt and Chippenham, at a higher fare and normally slower. Two morning auto-trains connected into expresses at Patney to provide Devizes–Paddington journeys of 2 hours 5 minutes in June 1939, about twenty minutes quicker than by the direct up trains.

FREIGHT TRAFFIC

The *Devizes Gazette* for 9 October 1902 commented that, even with the diversion of through trains over the new Lavington line, freight traffic to and from Devizes was far heavier than it used to be. In 1904 its goods yard had a ten-ton yard crane, more powerful than those at Chippenham, Marlborough, Newbury or even Swindon goods depots.[1] Just before the First World War, railway horse drays and lorries based at Devizes were busy collecting and delivering in the town. Outward traffic included meat, sent in ventilated vans to Smithfield; tobacco from Messrs Anstie; wool to mills in Yorkshire; hay and corn. Inward freight included groceries; fruit and vegetables; pigs for the Central Wilts Bacon Factory, driven on foot from the station to the slaughterhouse. A local businessman used to sponsor a Christmas dinner for local railwaymen in recognition of their importance to the town's economy.[3]

Seend gained a new importance in 1905 after a fresh attempt to exploit nearby iron ore deposits. The *Wilts Chronicle* for 19 August 1905 commented that calcined ore was being despatched daily to South Wales for trial blastings. By November the

11. Devizes station in about 1930, looking towards Holt. (Mowat Collection)

12. Holt Junction station in about 1920, looking towards the junction of the Devizes and Chippenham lines. (Mowat Collection)

results had been favourable enough to justify the laying of a new reception siding at Seend station. Although only forty tons of ore per day was railed from Seend initially, the promoters envisaged an increase with improved handling facilities including a tramway from the opencast site to the station.[5]

Although the ore proved uncompetitive and mining soon ceased, Seend station was considerably enlarged.

During the 1926 General Strike the GWR gave very high priority to maintaining the supply of milk by train to London. On 10 May, a 9.20 am Paddington-Weymouth milk empties conveying churns for stations including Devizes, Seend, Bromham Halt and Holt, appears to have been the only train scheduled to run over the branch. Two days later the GWR claimed to be running 45 percent of their services, but only a 5.35 pm Westbury-Savernake milk train and one passenger train from Reading to Trowbridge and back appear to have run via Devizes.[6]

REFERENCES

1. H. I. Quayle, op. cit.
2. G.W.R. Excursion Programmes.
3. T. J. Gaylard, 'When Rail Linked Town with a Big World Beyond', *Wiltshire Gazette & Herald*, 3.8.1967.
4. Railway Clearing House, *Handbook of Railway Stations* 1904. Reprinted David & Charles, 1970.
5. *Wilts Chronicle*, 11.11.1905.
6. G.W.R. General Strike papers. Public Record Office, ref. Rail 253/451.

FIVE

World War Two

The Second World War brought a new importance to the branch, as the need to utilise every available through route brought a great deal of long-distance freight traffic over it. Trains of sixty or seventy wagons in the down direction, stopping at Devizes to take water and at Seend for token exchange, became common. The board at the west end of Devizes station near the level crossing, reminding 'All Down Goods and Mineral trains to Stop Dead here' (at the summit of Caen Hill bank), was particularly relevant for the heavy trains of tanks and military supplies using the line at this time. To maximise line capacity, both Devizes and Seend signalboxes were open continuously. Sometimes a freight train might be recessed in Seend refuge siding for eight to ten hours if there was no spare path on the branch for it.

As railwaymen not in Reserved Occupations were called up, women were recruited to take over some of their posts. Three women came to work in Devizes goods shed, packing and unloading. Mrs Sarah Topp, whose brother was a Checker in the yard, started work in 1940 with hours of 8.00 am - 5.00 pm five days of the week and 8.00 am - 12.00 noon on Saturdays; tea breaks were sometimes shared with the Permanent Way gang, unofficially. Shunting, still performed by men, took place well outside these hours. Mrs Topp recalls a happy, hard-working atmosphere.

At this time Devizes goods yard had two horse drays for collection and delivery in the town, while a lorry collected supplies daily for the newly-established US Army camps at Prince Maurice and Waller barracks. Devizes station also employed female ticket collectors and two female booking clerks, a Mrs Chapple and a Miss Barkham; Miss K. Bishop, daughter of a Devizes guard, joined the staff as a booking clerk in 1940. The staff at Devizes, excluding PW and Signalling & Telegraph gangs was then thirty-five strong, consisting of:

1 Station Master	4 Platform Porters
3 Booking Clerks	1 Parcels Drayman
1 Parcels Clerk	4 Lorry / Dray Drivers
6 Goods Clerks	1 Checker
2 Foremen	1 Weighbridge Lad
2 Shunters	1 Goods Foreman
3 Signalmen	4 Goods Loaders
1 Level Crossing Keeper	

Next in command to the Station Master was the Chief Goods Clerk, perhaps a reflection of the volume of freight handled.

Seend station became very much a family affair when the wife of Leading Porter Robert Weston became one of two signalwomen there – it being the general practice to put women in charge of smaller boxes where possible. Their son Peter joined the staff as a Junior Clerk in 1943, and it was not uncommon for the family breakfast to be cooked in the signalbox. Seend then boasted a staff of ten:

1 Station Master	2 Porters
3 Signalpersons	1 Lad Porter
1 Checker	2 Clerks

Collection and delivery at Devizes of parcels sent by passenger train was still by horse dray at the time war broke out. This was mainly a town area delivery, recalls Jack Tottle, a clerk at the time. The station had to contact the GWR's Horse Department at Reading when the horse went lame. Petrol rationing put many railway lorries out of action, so two drays were also used for goods deliveries from Devizes. The railway stables had been taken over by Messrs Bibby's the agricultural merchants, so the GWR had to rent stables in the White Lion. Tom Newton, later a signalman at Devizes, started with the GWR as a horse driver there. 'The men used to think the world of the horses when they had got used to them,' recalls Miss Bishop.

Mrs Topp remembers Devizes goods shed handling five or six wagons a day at this time, in addition to scores unloaded in the yards. Army reservists staying for a fortnight's camp were accompanied by tanks and lorries; these arrived on flat wagons handled in the bay at the west end of the up platform. Large numbers of servicemen stationed in and near Devizes, at RAF Melksham and Keevil US Air Force bases, generated freight traffic in the form of provisions, the latter two camps receiving it via Seend station. The war also stimulated freight traffic originating on the branch. The NAAFI used to buy vegetables from growers whose produce was sent to numerous places from Seend and Bromham. Seend continued to send milk churns to West Ealing by passenger train.

Terry Gaylard, in one of his articles for the *Wiltshire Gazette,* has described how shocked Dunkirk evacuees detrained at Devizes. 'They presented a dishevelled, pitiful sight as they wandered around the town, lucky to be alive.'[1] Equally pathetic arrivals from 1944 onwards were German prisoners-of-war en route to a de-lousing centre at Roundway barracks. Very poorly dressed, sometimes in their underpants or barefoot, they were marched from the station in fours. By all accounts, the American guards were rough in their handling of the prisoners. Terry Gaylard has estimated that over a million Allied troops and 100,000 German prisoners passed through the station during the war. Trains also brought evacuees to Devizes, from London, soon after the war broke out.

With troops and evacuees swelling the local population, there was a greatly-increased demand for long distance travel. With petrol rationed, rail travel boomed. Prior to the war, a Passimeter had been installed in Devizes station entrance hall. This was a box in the centre of the booking hall with a wooden base but glazed from about four feet above the ground. Peter Weston remembers it being in use by 1937. From it the booking clerk would sell tickets to intending passengers through one window and inspect the tickets of detraining passengers through the other. The clerk operated mechanical arms controlling the entry and exit queues, as well as having to handle enquiries and do his bookkeeping when he could. The virtue, from Management's viewpoint, was that the device eliminated the need for a ticket collector but, as Jack Tottle recalls, it was the very opposite of privacy. To work under such conditions might make one feel like an animal being peered at in a zoo! The Passimeter also contained stocks of excess tickets, to cater for passengers arriving from Pans Lane and Semington Halts, which had no ticket offices.

At this time the Early turn for the booking clerk was 6.45 am to 3.45 pm with a lunch hour, after which he or she went into the Parcel Office. The Late turn was from 12.30 pm to 8.30 pm. The Passimeter was not the only entrance and exit at the station because passengers getting off the last trains of the evening (in 1939 these were the 10.00 pm Trowbridge–Pans Lane and 10.36 pm return) used a gate near the signalbox when the booking hall was closed.

Naturally, the Passimeter, intended for stations with relatively small passenger flows, was too cumbersome to deal with the volume of servicemen using the station and was removed. Back in the Booking Office proper, clerks now had more privacy, though no shortage of enquiries from conscripts planning journeys home on leave.

Devizes Booking Office began to issue very many Government rate single and return tickets for postings. To cope with demand, Seend was allowed to use over-stamped single ticket stock for Forces returns. One wonders whether BR's auditors would approve of such resourceful expediency today! Probably the best patronised trains at Seend were Friday leave specials to London, returning on Sunday; some were run primarily for personnel at RAF Melksham.

Among the trains most popular with civilian passengers were the early morning Reading–Bristol semi-fast, reaching Devizes around 10.00 am and bringing in shoppers from Pewsey Vale, particularly on market days; the 7.20 am Trowbridge–Paddington train and the 2.45 pm Paddington–Weston-super-Mare. Both the latter trains ceased running for part of the war as an economy measure. The 7.20 am Trowbridge was withdrawn when an Emergency Timetable commenced on 25 September 1939; this and the 6.25 am Trowbridge–Patney auto-train were replaced by a 6.30 am Trowbridge–Reading stopper, leaving Devizes at 7.00 am. However, the next timetable, starting in February 1940, restored the two early morning up trains.

Also reinstated then was the 2.45 pm ex-Paddington, but not as an express; it began calling everywhere between Newbury and Devizes (reached at 5.11 pm) including Pans Lane Halt. However, the train was again withdrawn in the October 1941 service, when the branch had no down train between the 2.05 pm from Newbury (due Devizes about 3.00 pm) and the 6.30 pm Devizes–Westbury auto-train.

Pans Lane Halt appears to have been temporarily closed with effect from 6 October 1941; no trains are shown as calling there in the timetable effective from that date, nor in the May 1944 service. Until the former date the evening auto-trains from Trowbridge had terminated at the halt, but now went no further than Devizes. In the early part of the war, the two down Sunday trains had set down passengers at Pans Lane on request to the Guard. By May 1944 a third down train was running to Devizes on Sundays; the 5.45 pm Paddington–Trowbridge now detached a portion at Reading. The main train reached Devizes at 8.42 pm but the rear portion did not arrive until 9.10 pm. Neither portion called at any other station on the branch.

The late morning Bristol–Reading train (a through service to London until September 1939) was popular with Seend passengers going to Devizes market on Thursdays at a third class fare of 4½d single, 6d return. US airmen from Keevil made great use of Seend station for afternoon trips into Devizes, using the

Bristol–Reading semi-fast or the Trowbridge–Patney auto-train. Peter Weston recalls occasions when Seend might issue as many as 100 tickets for one Saturday afternoon train.

As a result of the blackout, it was not uncommon for passengers to walk off the platform edges at Seend, so white lines were subsequently painted along it. At Devizes, where the globes enclosing the gas lamps on the platforms were blacked out for three-quarters of the way, it was the normal practice to have every other light lit when the station was in use; those on the island platform were extinguished completely when it was not being used.

REFERENCE
1. T. J. Gaylard, 'What's left of those Halcyon Railway Days?', in the *Wiltshire Gazette & Herald*, 3.1.1980.

13. Devizes station in the early 1950s, looking from the tunnel mouth. (Author's Collection)

SIX

Late Great Western, Early British Railways

Demobilisation resulted in the women railway workers being gradually given their notice, although single women were allowed to remain in employment for longer, e.g. Devizes had a female Goods Packer until 1948. The GWR's 1946/7 winter service still utilised Women Travelling Porters and Guards, based at Trowbridge. A Late turn for a Woman Travelling Porter (2.30 pm–10.30 pm) required her to join the 1.50 pm Weston-super-Mare–Reading (via Devizes) train at Bradford-on-Avon and travel with it to Newbury, whence she returned on the Trowbridge portion of the 6.00 pm from Paddington. One of her colleagues worked an Early turn on the 7.15 am Trowbridge–Paddington as far as Reading, followed by the 9.43 am ex-Reading which she left at Seend to catch the 11.22 am Bristol–Reading back to Newbury. Her final duty over the branch was with the lunchtime Reading–Westbury train.

Women also worked from Trowbridge as Guards on branch auto-trains; two were rostered from 6.15 am–2.15 pm to work the morning cycle of auto-trains between Trowbridge, Devizes, Patney and Warminster. A Late turn Woman Passenger Guard booked on at 3.20 pm; her duties included the commuter train between Trowbridge (5.52 pm), Devizes and return, also the late evening train to Devizes and back.

The longer distance passenger trains at this time had male Guards, assisted by Women Travelling Porters. Guards from Reading worked the Reading–Bristol semi-fasts, among other trains through Devizes although the 12.43 pm (SX) Reading–Westbury was rostered for a Frome Guard.

A Travelling Parcels Porter worked with the Sunday evening Trowbridge–Paddington train as far as Savernake, returning to Trowbridge on the 7.05 pm ex-Reading (the rear four coaches of the 5.40 pm Paddington–Trowbridge).[1]

During the early 1950s, Messrs Anstie, the Devizes snuff and tobacco manufacturer, was one of the line's biggest parcel customers. Ironically this sometimes made life easier for the Late Turn Clerk in Devizes Booking Office, if he was a Bristol District Relief Clerk, liable to be sent to work at stations as far apart as Cheddar, Calne, Cirencester, Devizes, Pilning and Swindon. Naturally, Clerks working a long way from home or from their next duty aimed at catching the last or most convenient train home if they could. The Late Turn Clerk at Devizes had to book the 8.35 pm train to Trowbridge, detached at Newbury from the 6.00 pm Paddington–Weymouth. As this train normally ran into the island platform, it could be a bit of a sweat to cash up, lock the safe and office, sprint over the footbridge and on to the train. However, the large number of tobacco parcels frequently loaded on to this train saved the day for the Clerk. An alternative, particularly if he was Late turn at Devizes one day and Early the next, was to sleep the night in the Parcels Office (with police permission); but rats not uncommonly scuttled across

14. Station Master S. W. Bray in about 1952. (Author's Collection)

its counter in the night and at least one Clerk felt happier to sleep on a camp bed than to use the floor.

The station itself had no regular cat, although the goods yard did. Rats were often found in the goods yard, recalls Alan Mead, a Clerk at Devizes Goods and Booking Offices from 1947-54.

On one occasion the railway rat catcher was called in and poison put down. Then a vile stench became noticeable – 'you could smell it in the goods office several days later'. This was traced to the loading bay, at the west end of the up platform, where fire buckets were found to be full of dead rats. The poison had dried up their throats and they had jumped up for water, thereby hastening their deaths.

Devizes now boasted a Class 1 Station Master. During the war, Station Master O'Donoghue had his job upgraded on the basis of the heavy military traffic. He was succeeded in 1948 by Sidney Bray, previously Station Master at Bridport, and grandfather of the author. His hours were approximately 9.00 am-5.00 pm with an hour for lunch. When the Station Master was on holiday his duties were covered by a Relief SM or by the Chief Goods Clerk, then a Mr Harding who later became Station Master at Lavington.

15. A group of station staff at Devizes, c1950. From left: Station Master Sidney Bray, Station Foreman Mr Bond, Tommy Newton and Joe Giddings. (Author's Collection)

Freight traffic at Devizes remained heavy. Inward traffic included coal, oil and military provisions; also live pigs for the Wiltshire Bacon factory. Bacon was sent to Cardiff every Monday, recalls Miss Bishop. Also sent to South Wales were pit props from Messrs Chivers, the Devizes building firm, and hay and straw for pit ponies. Most of the snuff and tobacco sent by rail went by passenger train. Jack Scown, Goods Cartage Clerk at Devizes from 1947-51, remembers working till 8.00 pm some days dealing with invoices for Messrs Anstie and the Wiltshire Bacon Company. There was regular horse traffic until the late 1950s, provided by Devizes Horse Fair held twice yearly on the town green. Cattle traffic was also heavy until about that time.

PASSENGER TRAIN SERVICES

Weekday services in the early BR years comprised about twenty departures daily from Devizes. Nearly half of these were auto-trains, not all of which went the full length of the branch. The auto-trains were third class only and usually called at all stations and halts, whereas the longer distance trains, starting or terminating at London, Bristol, Reading or Newbury tended to omit the halts and in some cases Seend as well. The 2.35 pm Paddington-Weston, running on a slightly slower schedule than pre-war, had no passenger stop on the branch except at Devizes, although it stopped at Seend for tablet exchange. Seend box had reverted to two shifts after the war. When it was in use (from 6.00 am-10.00 pm, weekdays only) the Holt–Seend and Seend–Devizes sections were worked by tablets, which were staffs about two feet long with a spring-loaded loop on the end. At times when Seend box was switched out, Holt–Devizes and Devizes–Patney were worked by electric token.

16. 7924 *Thornycroft Hall* brings the 2.35 pm Paddington–Weston-super-Mare into Devizes, August 1956. (P. Strong)

This dual system was to prevent confusion which might arise if signalmen had two separate sets of tokens.

Trains originating at London, Reading or Newbury provided seven of the eleven down weekday passenger services in the late GWR and early BR period. They were usually worked by 'Hall' 4-6-0s or 43XX 2-6-0s from Reading or Westbury sheds.[2] Indeed, stopping trains heading west on the main line from Newbury still tended to run via Devizes rather than via Lavington, reflecting the earlier role of the main line as a Reading–Trowbridge route.

The 2.35 pm from Paddington was still the fastest service to Devizes from the capital though it took over four hours from London to Weston, about an hour slower than via Swindon. Businessmen returning to Bristol, seeing it labelled at Paddington as a through service, would rush to catch this train and later become confused as it passed unfamiliar stations. The train detached a portion at Newbury (four of its ten coaches in Winter 1946/7) which formed a stopping train via Devizes to Bristol in 1946/7. However, the stopper terminated at Westbury by 1949. In the final GWR days, this down Newbury stopper was retimed to give a half-hour at Devizes, where it departed after the arrival of the commuters' auto-train from Westbury. This arrangement continued after Nationalisation. Its effect was that Devizes had no westbound passenger departure between the 2.35 pm Paddington (4.41 pm from Devizes in 1952/3), and the Newbury–Westbury service leaving just after 6.20 pm. So although the 8.00 am Trowbridge–Patney auto-train could bring

17. 0-6-0PT 5410 brings the 6.25 am Trowbridge–Patney into Devizes in June 1959. Note the box van at rear. (P. Strong)

commuters into Devizes, the town had no suitable train to take them home to Seend, Holt, etc., after finishing work about 5.00–5.30 pm. Before the war, the 4.33 pm stopper from Newbury did provide a suitable return service, leaving Devizes at 5.42 pm in July 1938 for instance. The opposite commuter flow, however, was catered for by the 8.05 am Devizes–Warminster and the 5.40 pm Westbury–Devizes. This probably reflected the greater availability of office jobs in West Wiltshire, particularly in Trowbridge.

Whereas the down weekday trains tended to be long distance services, the up trains provided more of a branch line service, particularly in the mornings when four of the five eastbound departures from Devizes were auto-trains to Patney, where they connected for Newbury or London with trains that had come from places west via Lavington, e.g. the 8.00 am from Trowbridge connected smartly at Patney with a Frome–Paddington express.

Weekday mornings witnessed an auto-train shuttle between Devizes and Patney. The first passenger train on the branch, the 6.25 am from Trowbridge, arrived at Devizes with newspapers and fish, unloaded by the Early turn Shunter or Porters, and then ran to Patney before returning to Devizes. After being crossed there by the Trowbridge–London through train, it formed an all stations service to Warminster, (8.05 am ex-Devizes for many years) and itself crossed the 8.00 am ex-Trowbridge at Seend. At least one Devizes schoolboy took advantage of this pathing to deliver meat for a butcher to a Women's Land Army Camp near Bromham Halt during the

44

18. Parcels are unloaded from the 6.25 am Trowbridge at Devizes, June 1959. (P. Strong)

war; catching the down stopper he had time to effect his errand and nip back for the up service.

The 8.00 am Trowbridge returned from Patney at 9.10 am in the Winter 1952/3 service after connecting out of an early Hungerford–Westbury train originating as the 4.30 am news train from Paddington. After reaching Devizes, the 9.10 am ex-Patney turned back again; its ability to proceed further west was blocked by the pick-up goods train leaving Holt at 9.10 am for Devizes and the 9.04 am Warminster–Devizes auto-train (return working of the 8.05 am Devizes auto). These auto-trains were hauled by 14XX or 54XX tank locos from Westbury shed. Later in the 1950s two-coach, non-corridor sets hauled by a 54XX or 57XX 0-6-0PT provided the short distance trains on the branch.

A phenomenon of the branch timetable in the early 1950s was a pair of trains waiting to leave Devizes in opposite directions for the same destination. In 1952/3 the 1.50 pm Newbury–Westbury lingered at Devizes for seventeen minutes to cross the 2.40 pm Trowbridge–Patney auto-train. On arrival at Patney the latter formed a service to Lavington and Westbury, which it reached ten minutes before the advertised through train. Alan Mead recalls that fares from Devizes to Westbury via Patney were higher, officially, than via Holt, although public timetables quoted several connections between Devizes and places to its west via Patney.

Among summer Saturday variations on the normal weekday timetable was a Reading–Weymouth semi-fast in place of the mid-morning Reading–Westbury stopper. In August 1954, the 9.40 am Reading–Weymouth (Saturdays) reached Devizes at 11.03 am, compared with an 11.45 am arrival of the 9.46 am from Reading in the week. After Devizes, the Weymouth train was non-stop to Holt,

45

19. A 57XX pannier tank prepares to leave Devizes with the 6.45pm to Westbury. (P. Strong)

20. 3735 in the loop platform at Patney with the 11.35 am stopper to Westbury via Devizes, January 1961. (P. Strong)

reaching its destination at 1.27 pm. This popular train catered for people taking their annual holidays at a time when rail had the lion's share of this market; but not for the day tripper, whose last train left Weymouth soon after 4.00 pm. The sensible train for a day trip to Weymouth was the 8.05 am Devizes, changing at Westbury, but the lack of cheap day fares was a deterrent.

Long day trips to places west of Devizes were hindered by the withdrawal of the late evening train from Trowbridge in 1951. It may have lost traffic with the abolition of petrol rationing but it had been popular with cinema goers; a few years later Alan Mead won £2 0s 0d for making a Staff Suggestion that it be reinstated on Wednesdays and Saturdays. Shortly before it was due to recommence, however, it fell victim again to a round of economy cuts. Before the train was axed one could leave Bristol for Devizes as late at 8.45 pm; thereafter one had to leave that city nearly three hours earlier to catch the 7.20 pm Trowbridge–Reading, now the latest up train.

Post-war services on Sundays were basically similar to their pre-war pattern of two trains each way. The additional evening train from Reading had been withdrawn by Autumn 1947, probably on account of demobilisation. The four trains in the 1949/50 Winter timetable served most stations between Reading and Patney but, apart from the up evening train calling at Seend, Devizes was the only stop on the branch. By the winter of 1952, Seend had lost this Sunday stop, its Station Master, and most of its staff, in an economy exercise. Together with Bromham, it now came under the control of the Devizes Station Master.

The Sunday trains were inconvenient for a day out to Bath, Bristol, or Weymouth as the first train to Trowbridge was not in Devizes until about noon. The evening train from Trowbridge was very popular with weekend visitors and servicemen, joining at Devizes. They detrained at Savernake where it was shunted clear of an up express connecting there for Reading and London. In the immediate post-war period it was a main link between people with families in Devizes and jobs in the Home Counties, among them my parents returning to Reading after a weekend with my grandparents. Wives and sweethearts would be out in force for this train on Devizes up platform.

Because of the widely-spaced Sunday trains, signalmen and station staff at Devizes worked split shifts. As only one Porter was booked on in the early morning, the Booking Clerk would sometimes muck in and help load fish boxes or churns on to the up morning train (7.17 am from Devizes in 1949/50).

Evening excursions to London were a feature of the early 1950s. Terry Gaylard remembers Saturday departures from Devizes about 4.30 pm and the platform thronged with people. The trains were powered by 'Hall' or 'Grange' 4-6-0s and returned from Paddington about midnight.

Also popular were special trains to Newbury Racecourse, one of which used to run from Cardiff via Devizes with a buffet car. On race days in August 1957, for instance, this train called at Holt, Seend and Devizes (11.45 am). Alan Mead remembers racecourse specials doing good trade from a wide cross section of society at return fares of 10s 6d first class, 7s 0d second class from Devizes. On Saturdays they attracted people able to leave early from work that morning.

The lack of a suitable train home from Devizes for commuters living west of the town was influenced partly by the timing of the down pick-up goods returning to Westbury. In 1946/7 this left Devizes at 5.45 pm Mondays to Fridays, crossing at Seend with the 5.40 pm auto-train from Westbury. By the time Seend loop was removed in 1956, the goods left Devizes at 5.15 pm, crossing the up passenger train at Holt.

The early turn Shunter at Devizes used to catch the 8.05 am passenger train as far as Holt, where he joined the 9.10 am pick-up goods back to his home station. This up goods train ran six days a week and was often hauled by a 45XX 2-6-2 tank. This class and 57XX panniers, based at Westbury, were preferred to tender locos for this trip as even small tender engines such as 22XX 0-6-0s were liable to derail on a very sharp curve in the up goods yard at Devizes unless the loco ran over it with extra wagons attached.

The 9.10 am from Holt would set back in a refuge siding at Seend. Shunting the yard there might include large consignments of coke for RAF Melksham. Joe Giddings, a Shunter at Devizes at this time, recalls that shunting could seldom be completed in time to get the train clear of the 9.04 am Warminster-Devizes and 8.10 am Reading- Bristol passenger trains. It was not unknown for the goods train to remain in the refuge siding for as much as three hours.

Shunting at Bromham could also pose pathing problems for trains as the ground frames controlling its sidings did not allow a freight train to be berthed there while a passenger train was in the Seend-Devizes section. To ease matters the freight

21. 0-6-0PT 9628 shunts Devizes up yard, c1959. (P. Strong)

engine was allowed to run light from Devizes to Bromham for shunting in the after-noon; it returned light to Devizes before working the down goods trip. Nevertheless the up goods sometimes did not reach Devizes till around 1.00 pm.

After Seend loop was abolished, ground frames were installed there giving access to the yard. The ground frames were released by the Devizes–Holt electric token and allowed a freight or ballast train to be stabled there while a passenger train was between Holt and Devizes. Signalmen at the latter two stations had to ensure there was sufficient room in Seend yard before permitting an engine or train to work there.

In the late 1940s, the down pick-up goods might have forty or fifty wagons, but this was not an impossible load for a pannier or prairie tank loco, recalls Joe Giddings. The up train, however, was limited to twenty-eight Class 1 (coal) wagons between Holt and Seend and fourteen such wagons beyond Seend. 'It was asking for trouble on a wet day coming up the bank if you didn't keep to this load,' he recalled.

Two slow, long-distance freights also used the branch until the night shift at Devizes box was abolished, which appears to have been in the mid-1950s. In winter 1946 these were the 1.45 am Bristol East Depot–Reading and an identical departure from Reading to East Depot! The down train, which terminated at Holt Junction in its final years, shunted numerous goods yards west of Reading, and did not reach Devizes until 10.17 am in the 1946 service. The up freight reached Devizes about 4.00 am. Both trains detached wagons at Devizes and their tedious journeys made it difficult to get crews back to their home station inside one shift. They were worked by 'Double Home' Guards who lodged away from Devizes on alternate nights of a week.

One express freight booked over the line, though diverted via Lavington in later years, was the 8.05 pm Paddington–Bristol Kingsland Road. It had a booked stop at Devizes for water and at Seend to pin down wagon brakes.[1]

REFERENCES

1. GWR Service Timetable, 7.10.1946–4.5.1947.
2. S. Rocksborough-Smith, *Main Lines to the West,* Ian Allan, 1981.

POSTSCRIPT

Vic Tucker, for many years a Westbury District Relief Signalman, has recalled a conversation with Sidney Bray in the early 1950s about the corrugated iron waiting shelter at Bromham Halt, the walls of which were rusting at the bottom. My grand-father had made an official suggestion that the bottom nine inches or so of the walls be removed and replaced with 18 inch strips of new corrugated iron bolted to the rest of the building. He naturally thought this would cost less than a new shelter.

The suggestion was progressed but was costed, on the basis of direct labour, at no less than £365. 'I can still hear Mr Bray saying, "Three hundred and sixty-five pounds! I could buy a garden shed for twenty!"' recalls Vic Tucker.

49

SEVEN

Decline Sets In

The only visible feature at Devizes station to mark its Centenary in July 1957 was evidently a flower bed on the up platform. But the line was still being vigorously exploited by regular excursions. The very first rail excursion from Devizes had been an enormous train to Weymouth; the same destination was offered on several summer Sundays in 1957 when a 9.45 am train from Savernake provided trippers from Devizes (dep. 10.20 am), and Seend (10.30 am), with nearly eight hours at the seaside; 'change at Trowbridge in each direction' read the small print on handbills. Passengers were back in Devizes at 10.50 pm. Fares (second class) were 9/9d from Patney or Devizes, 9/3d from Seend; these were also offered on Monday 5 August using the 9.30 am service train from Devizes to Patney, changing also at Westbury. On this date the return trip departed Weymouth at 7.30 pm, with a special connection for Devizes at Trowbridge. Also offered that day were cheap fares to Weston-super-Mare – 11/6d from Devizes (dep. 7.55 am) and 10/9d from Seend (8.05 am), changing at Trowbridge both ways. Special late trains to get excursionists home to Devizes were provided on the Saturday (7 September) of Trowbridge British Legion Carnival, (on other nights the 7.20 pm Trowbridge-Reading was the latest service), and for Pewsey Carnival on 21 September. For the latter event, Holt, Seend and Devizes people could use the Bristol–Reading trains due off Devizes at 12.30 pm or 4.00 pm, or a 4.45 pm special from Trowbridge (5.50 pm from Devizes) which served the halts as well.

Return trains were the Devizes portion of the 6.00 pm from Paddington or an 11.10 pm Pewsey to Trowbridge special.

Fares for the Pewsey trip were 3/9d from Semington, 3/3d from Seend, 3/0d from Bromham, 2/6d from Devizes and 2/3d from Pans Lane. For Trowbridge Carnival, Devizes offered day returns by any train for 4/0d first class, 2/9d second class; fares from Seend were 2/6d and 1/8d respectively. Comparable second class prices, by any train any day, were introduced in November 1957, e.g. to Trowbridge from Devizes 3/0d from Seend 1/9d. Even cheaper tickets were available at or after 9.30 am. If the day tripper to Bath or Bristol waited for the 8.10 am ex-Reading (10.00 am from Devizes), he not only had a through train but a considerably lower fare, e.g. Seend–Bristol 5/0d compared with 7/3d on the early down train. This was logical pricing in that there was an incentive to fill up seats outside peak hours. Unless there were special attractions such as Bristol Eisteddfod, Farnborough Airshow, Ascot or Newbury Races, the range of cheap day destinations offered from Devizes branch stations was small – only Trowbridge, Bath and Bristol being advertised as such in a November 1957 handbill. Stations with a cheap day fare *to* Devizes appear to have been largely confined to places in West Wiltshire and Pewsey Vale which had offered Devizes Market Day fares before the First World

War. BR was fighting bus competition for local traffic rather than, as nowadays, car competition over longer distances.

But day trips to London *were* being increasingly promoted. Whereas in spring 1955, Devizes-London day return fares of 27/0d first class, 18/0d second class, using early morning trains were virtually confined to Wednesdays and Saturdays the same fares were offered in autumn 1957 every day except Mondays and Fridays. On permitted weekdays Devizes passengers could use either the direct 7.44 am departure or the 8.45 am, changing at Patney. Return to Devizes was permitted by the 2.35 pm or 6.00 pm from Paddington. Half-day trips to the capital had also been marketed using the 11.02 am Devizes-Patney, giving people 4¾ hours in London for a second class fare of 11/3d in spring 1955, on selected Wednesdays and Saturdays.

However, these efforts did not prevent a gradual loss of passengers as car and bus competition began to bite. The sharp cuts made in 'lightly loaded services' throughout the Western Region from 30 June 1958 were announced at very short notice; organisations in Devizes had little time to protest against the withdrawal of some of its most convenient trains. In particular the loss of the 8.06 am Trowbridge-Patney was deplored. It was claimed to be the most popular service from Devizes (departing 8.45 am) to London, at least for day trips, as many people considered the 7.44 am departure too early and the 11.02 am (not bringing one to Paddington until 1.15 pm) too late.[1] The 8.06 am from Trowbridge and the down commuter train from Devizes had been retimed to cross at Holt instead of Seend following the closure of the latter station's loop and signalbox on 10 June 1956.

Cutting out the 8.06 am Trowbridge also involved the disappearance of its next two workings, the 9.05 am Patney-Devizes (used by six schoolchildren at the time)[1] and 9.30 am return; Management could claim the saving of a train crew and set.

Two Reading-Westbury trains were axed in the Monday to Friday service, but a new local train ran from Patney at 11.35 am to Trowbridge in the times of the withdrawn 9.43 am from Reading. The afternoon Bristol-Reading train ceased to start from Weston-super-Mare, except on Saturdays. The long-established morning Bristol-Reading train now started from Trowbridge during the week, while the 8.10 am Reading-Bristol (SX) was also diverted to Trowbridge with a wait of some forty minutes for a connection to Bath and Bristol. These cuts began a trend towards shorter distance trains on the branch which became more marked with successive alterations. In 1959 the afternoon Bristol / Weston-Reading train began to start from Trowbridge instead. The 6.00 pm from Paddington ceased to run after the summer of 1960 and the last down train to Devizes on weekdays started from Newbury at 7.40 pm instead of being detached from the express there. When the 2.35 pm from Paddington was withdrawn in September 1961, Devizes lost its last through train to Bristol and its last weekday express from the capital. Its replacement was a 3.45 pm Reading-Trowbridge semi-fast, which lingered at Devizes from 5.12 pm to 5.35 pm to allow the down local freight to run clear of it.

By now the local authorities had sensed danger and made concerned, though constructive, noises about train services. A Devizes Rural District Council delegation met BR's Divisional Traffic Manager at Bristol in October 1961, but their pleas, for 'good trains for residents to get to Salisbury, Bath and Bristol' (e.g. for hospital visits) and a suggested diesel railcar shuttle via Westbury, Patney and Devizes

22. 11.35 am train to Devizes leaving Patney, formed by a single railcar, January 1960. This working later reverted to steam haulage. (P. Strong)

23. *Rhuddlan Castle* climbs away from Pans Lane Halt towards Patney. Note the two vans for parcels. (P. Strong)

connecting with expresses, cut no ice. The meeting evidently emphasised the gulf between local opinion desiring an improvement in train service and BR's wish to drastically reduce rural trains. Traffic Manager D. S. Hart claimed a one-coach railcar was uneconomic and held out no prospect of increasing local services, of which total closure in the next few years was 'a very distinct possibility'.[2]

BR's argument, foreshadowing the Beeching Report, was that people were increasingly using rail for long-distance rather than local journeys. They would not or could not see that travellers often needed to use branch lines as part of a longer rail journey. Unfortunately, the usefulness of the Devizes branch for this purpose was hindered not only by service cuts, but by BR's unwillingness to stop West of England expresses at Patney. Whereas in the mid-1950s the late morning Devizes–Patney stopper connected with an up Weymouth–London express, people using this branch train in winter 1960/1 had to change again at Newbury for London.

Withdrawal of Weymouth–Paddington through trains meant that the Lavington route now tended to be used by Devon and Cornwall expresses calling only at the larger intermediate stations.

Although the train service was now less useful to the travelling public, events of 22 August 1961 had demonstrated the value of the Devizes branch as a diversionary route. A landslip at Lydeway, on the main line west of Patney, blocked the Lavington route for several weeks; scores of expresses were diverted via Devizes and Holt, including the 'Torbay Express'. The expresses were mainly powered by 'Hall' or 'Castle' 4-6-0s, or 'Halls' piloting 'Warship' diesels. Paul Strong, who lived at Stert at the time, recalls a ballast train from near the landslip site being worked to Westbury via Devizes by 2-6-2T No.4567. The branch was used to capacity and a night shift operated again at Devizes signalbox, which for some years had closed at 9.30 pm and opened at 5.10 am on weekdays. *The Wiltshire Gazette* spoke of the normal weekday service of sixteen passenger and four freight trains at Devizes being more than doubled during the diversion.[3]

The episode created problems with twelve-coach trains too long for the loops at Devizes. To enable such trains to cross, the down train waited at the east end of Devizes tunnel while the up train ran into the tunnel to reverse into the straight siding at the west end of the station. Signals could not be pulled off for this manoeuvre of the up train because the down train held the Devizes–Patney token. So a pilot signalman controlled the up train by waving a green flag until it was back over the three-way point. Station Master Edward Major was quoted as saying 'the diversion has certainly put Devizes station on the map. This sort of thing has happened before. It is a jolly good escape route'.[3]

Ten years previously the branch had been used to re-route expresses from a summer landslip on the Lavington line, but the hopes now raised locally for the future of the branch were soon dashed. Diesel multiple units had taken over some of the passenger trains by the winter of 1961/2 including the last down train on weekdays, which became direct from Paddington at 6.05 pm to Westbury. It lingered at Newbury from 7.12 pm to 7.35 pm, enabling a connection to be made out of the 6.30 pm from Paddington. One could now leave the capital, to be in Devizes the same night, later than for many years though not equalling the 7.30 pm departure possible before the First World War. But the cuts of 5 March 1962 changed the face

24. 4950 *Patshull Hall* on a Trowbridge-Reading train climbing Caen Hill bank, 1962. (P. Strong)

25. The 11.35 train leaving Patney for Westbury via Devizes, January 1961. The double track in the foreground is the main Lavington line to Westbury. (P. Strong)

26. 6959 *Peatling Hall* approaches Devizes with a Trowbridge-Paddington train. (P. Strong)

of rail travel west of Newbury. Most local trains along the Kennet Valley now went no further west than Bedwyn, 20 miles from Devizes. Worse still the branch lost all its Sunday trains. Ironically the two up trains and the down evening train on Sundays were direct London services at the time, when it was claimed that the 5.40 pm (Sundays) Trowbridge-Paddington was the most popular train of the week![4] Devizes box had operated a split shift on Sundays: in 1961/2 it was open from 7.10 am to 8.00 am, 11.30 am to 12.30 pm and 4.30 pm to 9.30 pm.

Losing the Sunday trains killed weekend traffic, particularly as several useful trains on weekdays were also withdrawn – the 11.45 am Westbury-Reading, the late morning Reading-Westbury service off Devizes at 12.52 pm, the Saturday lunchtime Reading-Westbury train leaving Devizes at 3.18 pm, the 3.45 pm Reading-Trowbridge and the 7.20 pm ex-Trowbridge. Withdrawal of the last mentioned now meant that Devizes had no service to Reading or London after 4.04 pm. The garrison town now had little or no train service to suit soldiers on weekend leave. A year later Pewsey station which also lost its Sunday trains in March 1962, was claimed to have lost 80 percent of its passengers as a result.[5]

The tragedy of the 1962 cuts was that Devizes lost nine through trains linking it with London or Reading. Although the 4.36 pm Newbury-Westbury stopper now started back from Reading at 4.07 pm to compensate for losing the 3.45 pm Reading-Trowbridge, this could not disguise the large gaps in the branch time-table. Only three trains now went eastwards from Devizes: the 7.10 am Trowbridge-Paddington, the 11.10 am Devizes-Patney and the 3.35 pm Trowbridge-Reading.

27. A two-car DMU on the branch at Stert Junction. (P. Strong)

Nor were travellers to Devizes from the Home Counties spoilt for choice; a day trip from Paddington now meant leaving at 7.10 am to catch the remaining morning train from Reading (due Devizes at 9.58 am), now a DMU originating at Slough. One could only return straight away by the 11.10 am from Devizes or wait until 4.00 pm.

Not surprisingly, people who had cars deserted the branch for stations such as Chippenham which, in keeping with BR's policy of building up main line services, had a good choice of London trains. This perhaps explains the largely phlegmatic reaction in Devizes to the slashing of its train services. The town's Chamber of Commerce expressed the hope that if Devizes station were to close alternative services would be provided at Lavington. The Borough Council, which had contemplated a bus station being built opposite the railway station, now had second thoughts in view of the trend of fewer trains. Some members of Devizes Trades Council argued that railways should be subsidised as a social service, but Alderman Brian Tilley told them it was hypocritical for people to protest against the loss of facilities which they did not themselves use. He said some trains were carrying only three or four people between Trowbridge and Devizes.[6]

The cuts were a blow to people without cars and to local rail staff who lost Sunday pay.

In 1961 the branch had lost its last direct Bristol train, the 2.35 pm ex-Paddington. The Bristol trains had run via Devizes largely to familiarise train crews with the route in case it should be needed for diversions. Their withdrawal, together with the 1962 cuts, caused railwaymen to suspect that BR no longer saw a use for the line. Removing the longer distance trains was also interpreted as a Management plot to drive passengers off the branch. 'They took off the trains that people were using and then said the line wasn't being used,' said one local railwayman.

REFERENCES
1. *The Wiltshire Gazette & Herald* 26.6.1958.
2. Devizes RDC, Finance & General Purpose Committee minutes 30.10.1961.
3. *The Wiltshire Gazette & Herald* 24.8.1961.
4. Ibid, 15.3.1962.
5. Ibid, 28.3.1963.
6. Ibid, 1.3.1962.

EIGHT

The Last Years

A ray of hope for the line's future came later in 1962 with the running of a Blue Circle cement train from Kent to South Wales down the branch. The train was booked to leave Hoo Junction at 23.30 every night except Saturday and, after a change of crew at Reading, was due off Patney at 05.29 (nearly twenty minutes after Devizes signalbox opened). It was timetabled to call at Devizes for water and leave there at 06.12, with a further crew change at Holt, but according to Paul Strong it ran considerably later in practice, reaching Devizes around 07.15 and crossing with the Trowbridge–Paddington train. On certain mornings the cement train terminated at Bristol St Philips, otherwise it ran to Magor, near Severn Tunnel Junction. Some of the cement was used in construction work at Llanwern Power Station.

Motive power included Standard 9F 2-10-0s – probably the heaviest locos ever to use the branch; 28XX 2-8-0s; 'Hall' and 'Grange' 4-6-0s. Paul Strong recalls the train having some twenty cement wagons and two brake vans. The return train to Kent was booked to run via Swindon and did not use the branch.

28. A 9F 2-10-0 prepares to leave Devizes with the 23.30 Hoo Junction cement train. (P. Strong)

29. D7040 on the 07.10 Trowbridge–Paddington train entering Devizes where a 9F 2-10-0 waits with the down cement train. (P. Strong)

No improvements, however, were made to the branch passenger service. Seend was an unstaffed halt by September 1962, when the morning train to London ceased to call there. Robert Weston, who had held the fort at Seend on platform duties and issuing tickets, moved to Devizes as Level Crossing Keeper. (The level crossing gave coal lorries access to the down yard.)

Although Seend still had considerably more trains than the other three halts, its service to London was now practically non-existent. To connect into the Trowbridge–London train meant catching the 06.25 Trowbridge (Seend dep. 06.46), at an unlit station because its Tilley lamps were now lit by the Guard of that train. To make matters worse, one had to wait half an hour or so for the Paddington service at Devizes, where the 06.25 Trowbridge now terminated. Seend's only other up morning train, the 09.04 Warminster–Devizes stopper (09.44 from Seend in Winter 1962/3) involved three changes – at Devizes, Patney and Newbury – to reach the capital. Only an absolute devotee of rail travel would willingly make such inconvenient journeys!

When Devizes MP Percival Pott was quoted in *The Wiltshire Gazette* that autumn as predicting the complete closure of the branch, the newspaper commented 'this has raised not a whisper of protest'.[1] In an increasingly motorised age people were becoming lazy about consulting timetables. With the train service cut back at Devizes, one could not just turn up on spec and expect a train reasonably soon to one's destination. BR's policy of building up regular interval services at main line railheads such as Chippenham appealed to travellers who did not want

30. A DMU finds little custom at Seend, c1965. (P. Strong)

31. Seend station after removal of the goods yard. (P. Strong)

to be restricted in their choice of trains. At this time Chippenham had a dozen or so weekday trains to Paddington, mostly direct, compared with three trains (only one a through service) at Devizes.

When the Beeching Report was published in March 1963 it proposed closure of the Devizes branch plus Patney, Lavington, Holt Junction and many other Wiltshire stations. Devizes Trades Council organised a meeting in July to discuss the closure threat with the Borough and Rural District Councils. Not much hope was held out for keeping the branch passenger service but speakers still considered freight services justified, particularly in bad weather. Devizes RDC thought that at best BR would only agree to keep open one of the three staffed stations (Devizes, Lavington or Patney), in the Council's area and that this was more likely to be a main line station. As the Borough Council favoured Lavington the Rural Council followed suit, having previously preferred Patney.

Trains calling at Lavington were about as sparse as those serving Devizes but the former station still enjoyed a well patronised Sunday evening train to London. The main line itself was not threatened in the Beeching Report which is probably why local councillors pinned their hopes on retaining Lavington station to serve the Devizes area. The tendency to write off all branch line services as slow and inconvenient was often ill-informed. Commenting in *The Wiltshire Gazette* for 15 February 1964 that the travelling public had for years 'scorned' the facilities Devizes station had to offer, Terry Gaylard went on to suggest that few people were aware of what trains were still available.

He instanced the direct 07.23 train to London (06.58 Trowbridge) arriving 09.46; a good connection from the 08.03 Devizes at Westbury for Weymouth, reached at 10.28; and an afternoon express from Torquay, connecting at Westbury with the 17.45 stopper to Devizes. One could have added that Devizes still enjoyed the direct semi-fast (from Reading) to Weymouth on summer Saturdays, although this terminated at Westbury in 1965.

32. 4472 *Flying Scotsman* visiting the line on 19 October 1963 with a Paddington–Ilfracombe excursion. (P. Strong)

The line's image must have suffered, though, from unimaginative services, seemingly planned with little regard for long distance connections. For instance, on peak Saturdays in summer 1962 the only afternoon train going east from Devizes terminated at Savernake, where one had to wait over an hour for a connection to Newbury, where a further change was necessary for London, reached four hours after leaving Devizes! There was no connection from London or even Newbury into the 11.35 Patney–Devizes–Westbury stopper which had replaced the 09.43 from Reading in 1958. With a patchy train service over the branch there was all the more need for well-planned connections.

The belief that closure was inevitable was reinforced by the decline of freight services. The down cement train appears to have ceased running by early 1964, when the freight trip from Trowbridge was running to Devizes five days a week. In March 1963, coal traffic handled at Devizes, brought by the latter train, was averaging 1,000 tons per month; local merchants Messrs Reeves, Maslem and Hinxman were then receiving up to sixteen wagon loads per week for delivery within a 15-mile radius of Devizes.[2]

In September 1964, the final timetable showing freight services over the branch, the goods train was rostered for a 57XX pannier tank. Leaving Westbury yard at 05.12, the train attached wagons at Trowbridge and was due at Devizes 06.20, half an hour before the first passenger train. On Mondays, Wednesdays and Fridays it was booked to run through to Woodborough before returning to Devizes at 08.25 for shunting. Departure back to Westbury was at 10.35 (11.00 Tuesdays and Thursdays). The loco was due back on Westbury shed within eight hours of its crew

33. 3735 hauls the down pick up goods towards Patney at Stert, summer 1963. (P. Strong)

34. Pick-up goods between Devizes and Patney, c1963. (P. Strong)

35. Pick-up goods train in the south face of the island platform, 1964. Devizes shunter Joe Giddings is second from right. (P. Strong)

booking on at about 04.00. The freight ran for the last time on 30 October 1964, hauled by 0-6-0PT No.3735. Closure had been brought about by BR's policy of concentrating freight traffic at the larger depots. Freight for Devizes was now handled at Chippenham, although the depot there has itself since closed.

Withdrawal of freight made more than half of the Devizes station staff redundant. In February 1964 a staff of twenty had included twelve in the goods department, plus the Station Master, two Leading Porters, two Signalmen, a Booking Clerk, Level Crossing Keeper and a Shunter.

Shortly before freight services ceased, BR published formal closure proposals for the branch passenger service and for all intermediate stations on the main line between Pewsey – now regarded by BR as the future railhead for mid-Wiltshire – and Westbury. Devizes RDC resolved that if it could not prevent the entire closure it should aim at keeping Lavington open. It wrote to the Borough Council and local parishes suggesting a joint case of objection. Send Parish Council declined to object, saying very few villagers relied on the railway.[3] (This was not surprising in view of its train service, the inconveniently sited station, and much more frequent buses.) The County Council took a wider view, objecting to the closure as a whole in the hope of getting a better service from Devizes and Pewsey to serve the mid-Wilts area.

There was certainly room for improvement, as objectors pointed out at the public inquiry into the closure proposal, held at Devizes Town Hall on 5 April 1965. The Transport Users' Consultative Committee, which conducted the inquiry and

36. Trowbridge–Paddington train crosses the morning commuter train to Westbury at Devizes, spring 1965. (P. Strong)

37. Signalman Bert Clack throws the Devizes–Holt token to the driver of the 18.30 train to Westbury, June 1965. (P. Strong)

reported its findings to the Minister of Transport for his decision, was only authorised to consider objections based on hardship the closure would cause to existing rail users. Naturally, there would be few users of an infrequent service with poor main line connections.

BR's public timetable for January–June 1965 showed Holt–Patney and Westbury –Reading on widely separated tables with no indication that the 06.58 Trowbridge (07.23 Devizes) was a through London train. Of four down trains starting from Newbury, only the 19.36 to Devizes and Westbury had a good connection from Paddington leaving at 18.30.

One objector claimed that he could not reach Devizes from London until 13.38, and had therefore been unable to present his case at the TUCC inquiry which closed just after 13.00 hours. This arrival was via the 12.30 ex-Newbury, introduced in June 1964 and which in theory plugged a gap in main line connections caused by the 1962 cuts.

In fact, the opportunity was wasted by the very poor connection from London, involving an additional change at Reading and long delay at Newbury ($1\frac{3}{4}$ hours wait there in the 1965/6 service).

The ending of freight and retiming of passenger trains now meant that few trains needed to cross at Devizes. In the summer of 1965 its signalbox was closed; the passing loops and sidings were disconnected. The branch now became one section of plain track from Holt to Patney. Only the up platform at Devizes was now used. This economy coincided with the retirement of the two Signalmen.

The train service remained almost unchanged, however. The 06.25 Trowbridge ran as empty stock from Devizes to Patney, crossing the 06.58 Trowbridge there before running back empty to Devizes to form the down commuter train. The evening Westbury–Devizes commuter train continued as empty stock to Patney so as to cross the 17.36 ex-Newbury there instead of returning down the branch from Devizes.

Practically all the trains were now worked by DMUs and Devizes station staff were reduced to four. No longer having a Station Master, it came under the Area Manager at Chippenham.

THE AXE FALLS

With its lifted sidings and boarded up footbridge, Devizes station presented a forlorn appearance. The Transport Minister approved the closure proposal in December, claiming that the town was adequately served by Chippenham station and seeing no case for Lavington to remain open. Terry Gaylard commented soon afterwards in *The Wiltshire Gazette* that remaining trains serving Devizes were now nearly empty.

Closure was fixed for 18 April 1966, Saturday 16 April being the last actual day of service. Detonators greeted the three-car DMU forming the final Westbury–Devizes train at Holt and Sells Green. Rockets were fired at Bromham Halt. A crowd gathered at Devizes for its last train, the 19.36 Newbury–Westbury.

Holt and Patney signalboxes closed down with the branch but the line was to see more activity yet. On 2 June 1966 the Royal Train was stabled on the branch just east of Holt for the night. Its locomotives D.1010, *Western Campaigner* and D.1041 *Western Prince,* traversed the branch the next day although the stock remained at

38. A DMU waits to depart from Devizes on the last day of service, 16 April 1966. (P. Strong)

65

39. DMU entering Devizes on the last day of operation, 16 April 1966. (P. Strong)

Holt. The two signalboxes were specially reopened for the operation. The train headed west via Trowbridge.

A two-lever ground frame was installed at Holt to enable track lifting to commence westwards from Patney. The first demolition train, in late January 1967, was delayed by a landslip in the rock cutting between Devizes tunnel and Pans Lane. (Ironically, another landslip had delayed the opening of the original branch in 1857.)

In March the demolition contractor had possession of the line from Patney to Devizes; BR provided a train to remove materials thence to Westbury, hauled by a 'Hymek' or 'Warship' diesel. Most of the buildings at Devizes station were smashed up and the woodwork burnt.

Lifting was complete by the summer of 1967 except for a short stretch between Holt and Whaddon Bridge, still in situ in 1977 having been used in the early 1970s for wagon storage.[4] However, this rump had been removed by the early 1980s.

Most of the bridges were demolished one by one. The Fish Bridge was removed in February 1969, making way for road improvements. A year later the stone-arch Sleight Bridge defied nearly 300 sticks of gelignite and had to be broken up by an excavator. Surviving features include Seend platforms, Caen Hill embankment, the tunnel entrance and a small concrete bridge at Devizes station site. Perhaps the most curious of all, Devizes goods yard gates stand incongruously in Western Region cream paint outside a small estate on the yard site.

British Rail had relieved itself of a steeply graded line, with many earthworks, bridges and a tunnel, at the price of losing an alternative route between Bath and Reading. However, Hawkeridge curve at Westbury (opened in 1942) fulfills the same function of avoiding Swindon, without the physical constraints of the

66

40, 41, & 42. Devizes station shortly after closure. (P. Strong)

Devizes line. Had the new curve not been built, the Devizes branch might have survived, at least as a diversionary route. Indeed the overnight freight from Paddington to Bristol Kingsland Road was switched from the Devizes route to run via Hawkeridge in later years.

Today, Devizes, four times the size of Pewsey which enjoys Inter-City trains, is not well served by public transport. The few remaining buses to Chippenham take almost an hour, although the direct road distance is about ten miles. Buses to Pewsey are fewer still. In 1883 H. E. Medlicott, arguing for more frequent trains, claimed that Devizes was 'left on the shelf' by its train service; he said people were reluctant to visit the town because it took so long to reach. The same could be said if one does not have access to a car today. This reduction in accessibility cannot possibly be called progress.

REFERENCES
1. *The Wiltshire Gazette & Herald*, 15.11.1962.
2. Ibid, 28.3.1963.
3. E. Bradby, *Seend, A Wiltshire Village Past & Present*, Alan Sutton, 1981.
4. H. I. Quayle, op.cit.

41

42

43. D809 *Champion* at Devizes with demolition train, March 1967. (P. Strong)

69

44. Demolition contractor's loco at Devizes, March 1967. (P. Strong)

45. Demolition train at Devizes, March 1967. (P. Strong)

46. The end of the line. Lifting in progress between Patney and Devizes, March 1967. (P. Strong)

NINE

The Line Described

Leaving the Chippenham–Westbury line just north of Holt Junction station, the Devizes branch swung eastwards and about ¼ mile further on, crossed the River Avon by Whaddon Bridge. This was a GWR 'caisson' bridge built in the early 1880s to replace one of Brunel's wooden pile bridges. It had two river and two land spans.

The line then continued across flat countryside, keeping north of the Kennet & Avon Canal, and running on a low embankment, then through a short cutting near Whaddon Grove Farm. After a stretch of 1-in-66 rising gradient on a low embankment, the line reached Semington Halt (1m.61ch. from Holt) which stood above the west side of the A350 Chippenham–Westbury road which it crossed by Outmarsh Bridge, a three-span girder bridge on brick pillars. The same bridge also crossed the disused Wilts & Berks Canal. Semington Halt was convenient for RAF Melksham

47. The junction at Holt, April 1966. The Devizes branch curves to the right. (P. Strong)

48. Semington Halt, looking east. (Lens of Sutton)

about a mile away, although Seend station was almost as near the camp and had more choice of trains. The halt, opened on 1 October 1906, was a low platform on the up side and was rebuilt on 22 February 1909, the day that Bromham & Rowde Halt opened. The shelter, provided in July 1907, had a flat roof sloping backwards and was similar in design to the shelters at Avoncliff on the Bath–Westbury line. The low platform was built with the retractable steps of Railmotors in mind and virtually all the trains stopping there were all-stations trains from Westbury or Trowbridge to Devizes or Patney.

The line went almost dead straight east of the halt, passing south of RAF Melksham, before curving in a slightly north-easterly direction through three shallow cuttings, $\frac{1}{4}$ mile or so north of the Kennet & Avon Canal. From the second cutting the railway was straight for nearly two miles to Seend station (3m.75ch.), located on the west side of a bridge under a road between the A365 (Devizes–Melksham) road and Seend village. Mr Bradby has told how the station was originally to be sited further east but was built below Bolland's Hill to be nearer the ironworks that had just opened.[1]

The station at first had one platform on the north side but on 30 August 1908 a new loop, second platform and signalbox came into use. The new buildings were standard GWR designs for the period – the down waiting shelter of brick with a canopy resembled one standing at Bramley (Hants) today. A cast iron gents toilet stood on the up platform. The station does not appear to have collected or delivered freight and parcels, but in late Victorian times Jonah and George Rawlings ran a business carrying traffic between Seend station and village in a hand-truck.[1] During the last war, coal for RAF Melksham and stores for the USAF base at

49. 5416 prepares to run round before returning to Westbury with a passenger train one May evening in 1959. Note wooden signal posts. (P. Strong) -

50. A 'Hall' class loco prepares to leave Devizes with the Sunday lunchtime train to Westbury (ex-Reading), c1960. (P. Strong)

51. Seend station after removal of the platform loop, looking east. (P. Strong)

Keevil came by rail to Seend. Coal merchants at the station included Messrs Deverill, Doughty, Hillier and Parsons.

Various attempts, mostly short-lived, were made to exploit the local iron ore deposits south of the station, between 1856 and 1946. Traffic in partly-purified ores from Seend to Swansea Haematite Works began in 1905 and helped to justify the station improvements of 1908. But the traffic did not last long as Seend ores were too high in silica content to be competitive. During the Second World War a crushing plant at Seend ground oxide of iron. Some granules were mixed with sawdust before being brought to the station in Messrs S. H. Barter's lorries.

An official GWR plan of 1927 shows two loops at the station, one for the down platform; the other, running behind the down platform, was connected to the up platform line by two crossovers and fed three sidings. The westernmost of these, on the site of the original tram road from the ironworks, was the refuge siding for slow freight trains. Up freight trains such as the Holt–Devizes pick-up would run to the east end of the station and set back into the siding to allow passenger trains to pass. This movement was required, for instance, to keep the up pick-up goods clear of a Trowbridge–Devizes stopper and a Reading–Bristol semi-fast in the early 1950s.

At the east end of the up platform was a tablet catcher; the signalbox built to a typical GWR design (c.f. Yeovil Pen Mill) was near the west end of the down platform. The fireman of an up train would sling the Holt–Seend tablet on to the tablet catcher whilst grabbing the Seend–Devizes token from the machine. Peter Weston recalls the latter tablet being dropped one night in wartime and the section from

75

Seend to Devizes being paralysed until it was recovered from a hedge.

The long siding at the south side of the station was for general merchandise traffic, unloaded by local contractors.

SEEND TO DEVIZES

East of Seend began an almost continuous climb to Devizes. Bromham & Rowde Halt (5m.22ch.) was on the Devizes side of a bridge carrying a minor road to Bromham over the line, but the halt was between Sells Green and Martinslade, miles from either Bromham or Rowde. Opened in 1909, it consisted of a wooden platform on the south side with a Pagoda waiting shelter at the west end, goods checker's hut at the east end and a canopy between the two buildings. The station had much traffic in vegetables brought by lorry from Bromham, particularly sugar beet. The vegetable siding was at the east end of the station, as was the siding opened in 1941 to serve the sawmills of Messrs Partridge & Cox, later the Seend Electric Sawmill Co. Access to each siding was controlled by ground frame. Peter Weston recalls the sawmill being in full swing in the early postwar period.

Sugar beet traffic was so heavy in the 1940s and 1950s that, in view of the limited siding accommodation, each grower was allocated specific weeks for loading. For major growers the allotted periods might be staggered, e.g. he might be allowed to load one truck one week, none in the next, two in week three and so on, according to the quantity and destination; but hard frost which might prevent the beet from being dug out could play havoc with this system. During 1943-5 much of the beet went to Netherfield near Nottingham; in BR days it went mainly to the Kidderminster factory.

There was a coal merchant at the halt but the faster turnover of wagons at Seend, which had more siding space, meant that the merchant often preferred to unload his coal there.

52. Bromham & Rowde Halt, the sawmill is in the right background. (Lens of Sutton)

53. A 'Hall' crosses Foxhangers Bridge with an up train. (P. Strong)

The halt was manned until 1 November 1951 by a Goods Checker but had no clerical staff; its freight clerical work was done at Seend, the cash and documentation being sent down in the afternoon. Peter Weston recalls that timber from the sawmill siding was not weighed but its weight was calculated from the cubic measurement against tables of different timbers, as Bromham had no crane. By the time he came to Seend in 1943, the truck weighbridge (installed for the ironstone traffic) had gone so wagons from Bromham or Seend were often double-labelled. On one side of the label was the weighing station (frequently Bristol Kingsland Road for westbound traffic); on the other, the actual destination. The sawmill siding and ground frame were closed in May 1962; Seend and Bromham both closed to freight from 10 June 1963.

About half a mile further east, the line crossed the canal by Foxhangers Bridge after running on an embankment on the north side of the waterway. The three-span girder bridge on brick pillars is believed to have been a replacement for an earlier design of cylindrical pillars encased in concrete.[2] After two short cuttings the line began to rise more steeply and crossed the junction of the A361 Devizes–Bath road with Marsh Lane by means of the Fish Bridge, one of the line's best known landmarks, and so named because its tubular girders were shaped like a fish's belly, although these were replaced by more modern girders in 1901.

Terry Gaylard remembers it being noisy to travel over. The 160 feet long bridge rested on stone and brick abutments supporting embankments on either side. It has been suggested that one original proposal was for a 'fiendish looking' bridge of timber and wrought iron tie rods.[3]

This, the line's longest bridge, stood at the foot of Caen Hill embankment which rose towards Devizes for over a mile at 1-in-60. After a stretch of high embankment, in which a culvert bridge survives, the line went through a cutting and curved round in a slightly south-easterly direction towards Devizes castle, reaching its

77

54. A 'Hall' 4-6-0 takes a Trowbridge–Reading train up Caen Hill bank, 1962. (P. Strong)

55. 5940 *Whitbourne Hall* reaches the summit of the incline. Note the board 'All down goods and mineral trains to stop dead here'. (P. Strong)

summit of 1-in-52 near the prison buildings before entering the station.

This gradient was certainly taxing for locomotives and train crews. Bill Crosbie-Hill, recalling trains climbing this summit in wartime, has commented:

> With the right class of engine, in good mechanical condition ... a driver and fireman familiar with the route, a good head of steam after a sharp getaway from Seend, the ascent could be comfortably made.[4]

Terry Gaylard has recalled that 4-cylinder engines such as 'Star' and 'Castle' class 4-6-0s were more prone to trouble on this climb. Two-cylinder 4-6-0s of the 'Saint', 'Hall', 'Grange', and 'Manor' classes took more kindly to the trial. 'Star' class locos were particularly prone to slipping, perhaps because of their large driving wheels.

The sparse loco watering facilities between Holt and Reading – e.g. in the 1950s, there were no water cranes between Devizes and Savernake – encouraged the use of tender locos for the longer distance trains.

Bill Griffin, a Platelayer in the Devizes Permanent Way gang from 1928 to 1965, remembers the early morning Bristol–Reading freight train sometimes getting into difficulties on the bank and having to be divided. Banking engines were sometimes employed but were not allowed to be loose-coupled. In 1946/7 a shunting engine from Holt used to assist this freight to Devizes, shunt there for some twenty minutes and then return light. In October 1960 the Sectional Appendix to the Working Timetable stipulated that assisting engines of up freight and ECS trains were to be attached to the rear of the train at Holt and detached at Devizes by the Guard. Assisting engines for up passenger trains had to be attached in front. If the train was not booked to call at Holt the engine should be attached at Bradford-on-Avon. Drivers of banking engines were instructed to take great care over stretches of falling gradient 'so that the train engine alone pulls the train', also to exercise care in running from the summit of Caen Hill incline to the station.

DEVIZES STATION (8m.17ch.)

After removal of the overall roof before the First World War, the station layout consisted of two platforms, the down one an island, two platform loops and two goods yards. The up yard, carved out of a cliff face below the Convent, rose on a slight embankment above the running line at the west end of the station.

Most of the goods facilities were located in this yard, which was shunted by the loco of the Holt–Devizes pick-up freight; it ran light to Bromham if required to sort wagons there for collection on the down trip. In 1946/7 the light engine was due off Devizes at 3.45 pm, returning from Bromham at 4.07 pm to continue shunting at Devizes.

The goods shed was of Bath stone and had black wooden ends. The original goods office at the station end of the shed was also of stone but a brick extension was built above it, reached by an external spiral staircase. A red brick extension to the west of the shed had a cream wooden canopy. Immediately west of this were two loading sheds, one a cattle feed store with a corrugated roof, used by Messrs Silcock. The 6-ton yard crane was at the west end of the yard and had two gears according to the load and / or available manpower. Both this and the 1½-ton crane inside the goods shed were hand-operated.

At the station end of the yard was a cattle dock with two pens, adjacent to the end of the up station platform. A brick built weighbridge hut stood north of the cattle

56. Devizes station looking west. (Lens of Sutton)

57. Forecourt of Devizes station during demolition, March 1967. (P. Strong)

58. Devizes station looking east. (Lens of Sutton)

dock, near the wooden yard entrance gates. At the foot of the cliff was a long loading dock, served by a siding which had a headshunt at its eastern end until about 1960. The water tank was reached by steps from near the east end of this siding. Next to it was Messrs Bibby's cowcake store, built of brick and formerly stables; also two galvanised sheds used by Messrs Hinxman the coal merchant.

The up station platform, about 170 yards long, was occupied at its western end by the main station offices, part of the original building. The station building, entered from Station Road, contained in BR days (from west to east) gent's toilet, Station Master's office, parcels office, booking hall and ticket barrier, waiting room and ladies' rooms. It was built of Bath stone with slate roof and brick chimneys. A little to its east, just before the platform curved sharply towards the tunnel, was the signalbox of blue brick with a slate roof. It was kept impeccably clean by the late Rowley Reeves and Bert Clack, the last signalmen to work there. Between the signalbox and station offices was the footbridge, built of iron with wooden panelling and corrugated roof. The structure was painted cream, except for brown girders immediately above the running lines. At one time enamel advertisements adorned the steps. A little further along the platform a gate in the railings allowed access from Station Road for parcels lorries, mail vans and Messrs Anstie's tobacco consignments.

The island platform accommodation was two separate wooden waiting rooms under a typical GWR canopy. The south face of the island was not much used by passenger trains in BR days, except during diversions but it was a useful recess and often kept the branch pick-up freight train clear of passenger services.

DB-F

59. Devizes station looking west. (P. Strong)

60. Devizes signalbox. (P. Strong)

61. Devizes station, west end showing water crane on island platform. (P. Strong)

Water cranes stood at the London end of the up platform and the west end of the island. D. J. Fleming recalls that Devizes was popular as a watering point with train crews because the cranes, 'of a somewhat low pressure' gave one time to make tea![5] The low pressure was probably due to their being fed from the canal via the water tank. Men from Swindon and Westbury loco depots used to clear the feed pipe of weeds and debris. Alan Mead remembers a barge getting stuck for three weeks on the canal in 1949 damming up the railway's water supply for cranes and toilets. The drinking water tap at the Bristol end of the station was fed by a pipe from the Market Place.

The platform lines converged at the east end of the station in a three-way point straddling a small concrete bridge at the tunnel mouth. This point survived until 1965, although an official plan of 1927 shows two turnouts. The sharp curvature of the platforms meant that trains might be given Right Away via a porter when the Guard could not see the end of his train.

A siding from the down platform line crossed the up platform line just beyond the London end of the platforms and curved away from the direction of the tunnel to terminate further up Station Road. It served a wooden PW Inspector's office which had a slate roof, possibly the upper half of a former signalbox which stood at the tunnel mouth.

Two goods loops branched from the line serving the south face of the island platform. A long siding from the southernmost loop adjoined coal staithes and near its eastern end was an Anglo American oil depot, shown on plans as early as 1914. To its west were Shell-Mex and ROP oil storage depots.

The tunnel under Devizes castle had grey stone portals; those at the station end are now in use as a rifle range. After emerging from the 190-yard tunnel at the Patney end, the line went under a sleeper-built footbridge leading to St John's Churchyard, called Wooden Bridge even after rebuilding in concrete. After going under Hillworth Road bridge the line entered a rock cutting, passed under Salisbury Road bridge and reached Pans Lane Halt (8m.75ch.), a wooden platform on the down side with a corrugated iron shelter. It was opened on 4 March 1929, largely to serve Roundway Hospital (formerly the County Asylum). Unlike Semington, the platform was of normal height and a few longer distance trains called there. For most of its existence it appears that no trains called on Sundays. Steps led down from a gate on the road bridge to the halt. A whistle board at the Devizes end warned down trains of the approach to the tunnel.

The line, no longer in a cutting, now continued in a south-easterly direction, crossing a road to Sleight Farm by an arched stone bridge about half a mile from the halt.

The line went into a cutting near Stert village with a road overbridge at either end; after Stert it ran on an embankment and then passed over the A342 Andover road which soon afterwards crossed the converging main line. The two lines rubbed shoulders at Stert Junction, some twelve miles from Holt, but the branch continued on a descending embankment parallel with the Lavington route before the tracks actually merged at Patney station (13m.1ch.). Had it not been for the opening of the Lavington line is is doubtful whether a station would have been built at Patney (population 127 in 1901, declining to 85 in 1921).

62. Pans Lane Halt, looking east. (Lens of Sutton)

63. Patney & Chirton, looking west, between the wars. (Mowat Collection)

64. Patney & Chirton, looking east, about 1920. (Mowat Collection)

65. Patney signalbox, shortly after closure. (P. Strong)

The station was on the west side of the road from All Cannings to Chirton. Up branch trains used the outer face of the island platform, a loop useful for keeping a Devizes to Reading train clear of up expresses, as some stations between Patney and Newbury lacked loops for holding slower long distance trains. The station buildings were of red brick with slate roofs. The signalbox of brick and timber was at the west end of the down platform. Between the signalbox and the platforms were tablet catchers for branch trains not calling at Patney. The station was closed to freight from 19 May 1964, became unstaffed on 8 November 1965 and closed completely with the branch. The footbridge, minus its canopy, is the only surviving structure.

REFERENCES

1. E. Bradby, op.cit.
2. A. Vaughan, *A Pictorial Record of Great Western Architecture*, OPC.
3. 'A Last Look at Holt Junction', *Holt Magazine*, 1967.
4. W. Crosbie-Hill, 'Heyday at Devizes', quoted in *The Wiltshire Gazette & Herald*, 27 January 1983.
5. D. J. Fleming, *St Philip's Marsh, Memories of an Engine Shed*, Bradford Barton.

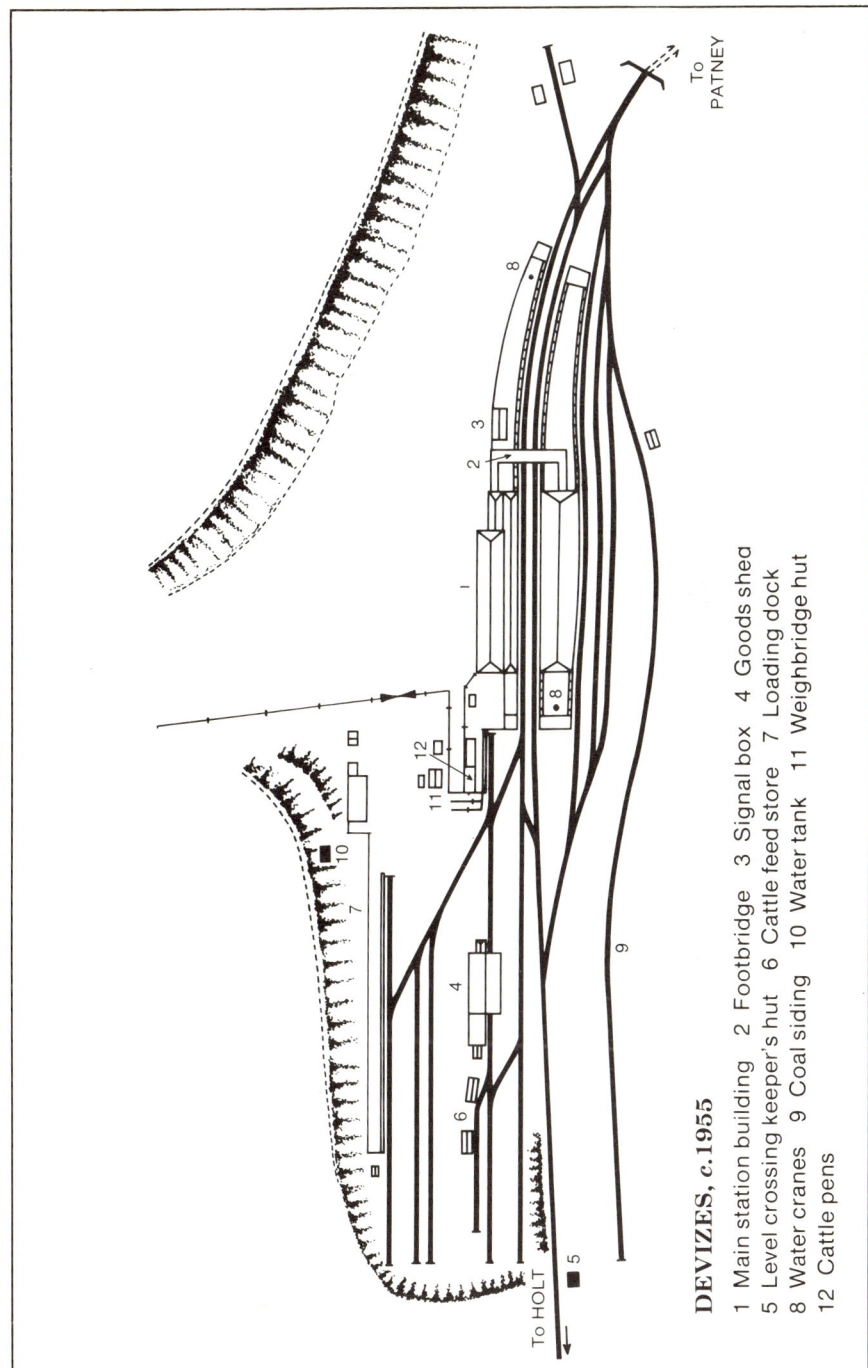

DEVIZES, c.1955

1 Main station building 2 Footbridge 3 Signal box 4 Goods shed
5 Level crossing keeper's hut 6 Cattle feed store 7 Loading dock
8 Water cranes 9 Coal siding 10 Water tank 11 Weighbridge hut
12 Cattle pens

To PATNEY
To HOLT

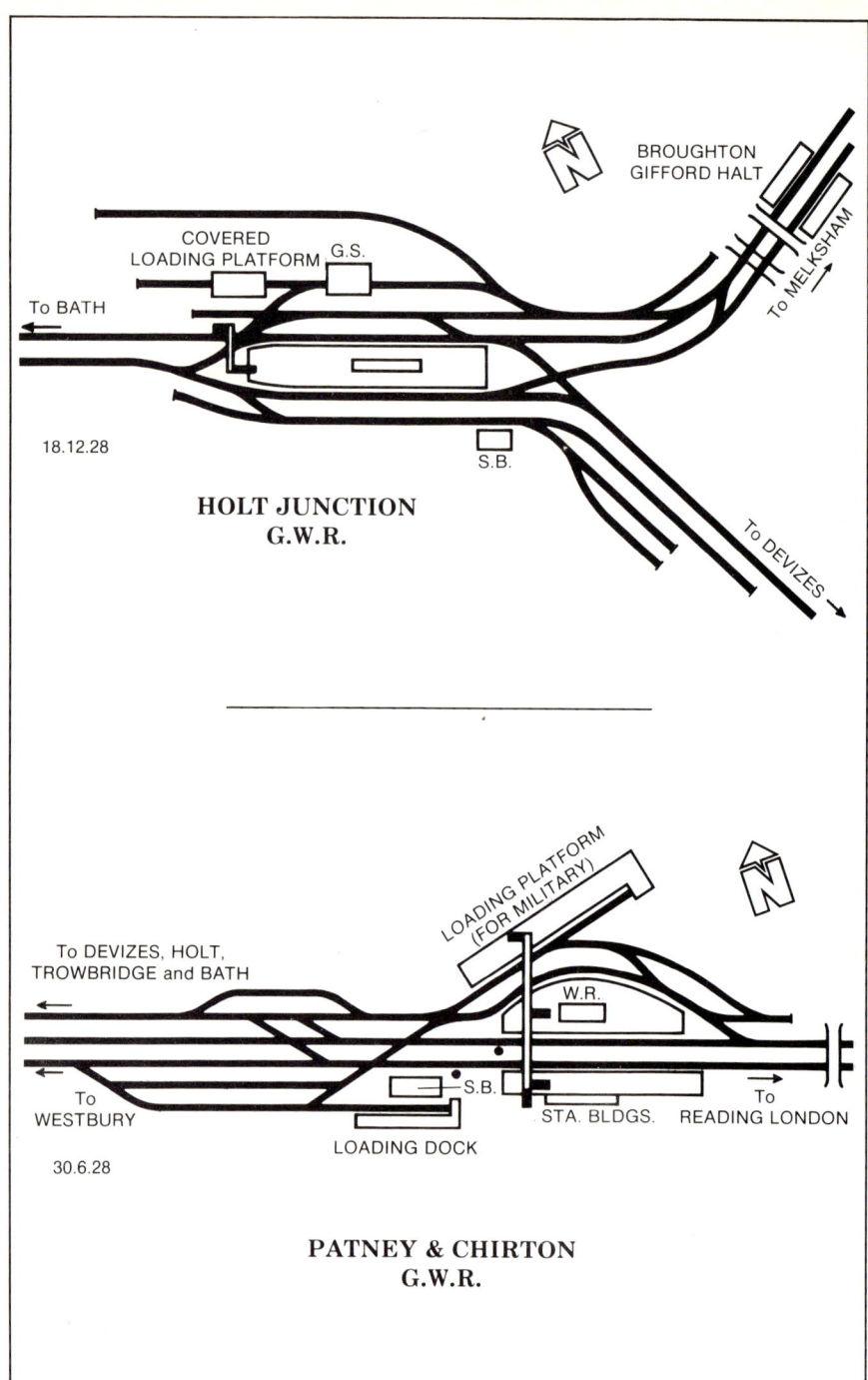

BROUGHTON GIFFORD HALT

COVERED LOADING PLATFORM

G.S.

To BATH

To MELKSHAM

18.12.28

S.B.

HOLT JUNCTION
G.W.R.

To DEVIZES

LOADING PLATFORM (FOR MILITARY)

W.R.

To DEVIZES, HOLT, TROWBRIDGE and BATH

To WESTBURY

S.B.

STA. BLDGS.

To READING LONDON

LOADING DOCK

30.6.28

PATNEY & CHIRTON
G.W.R.

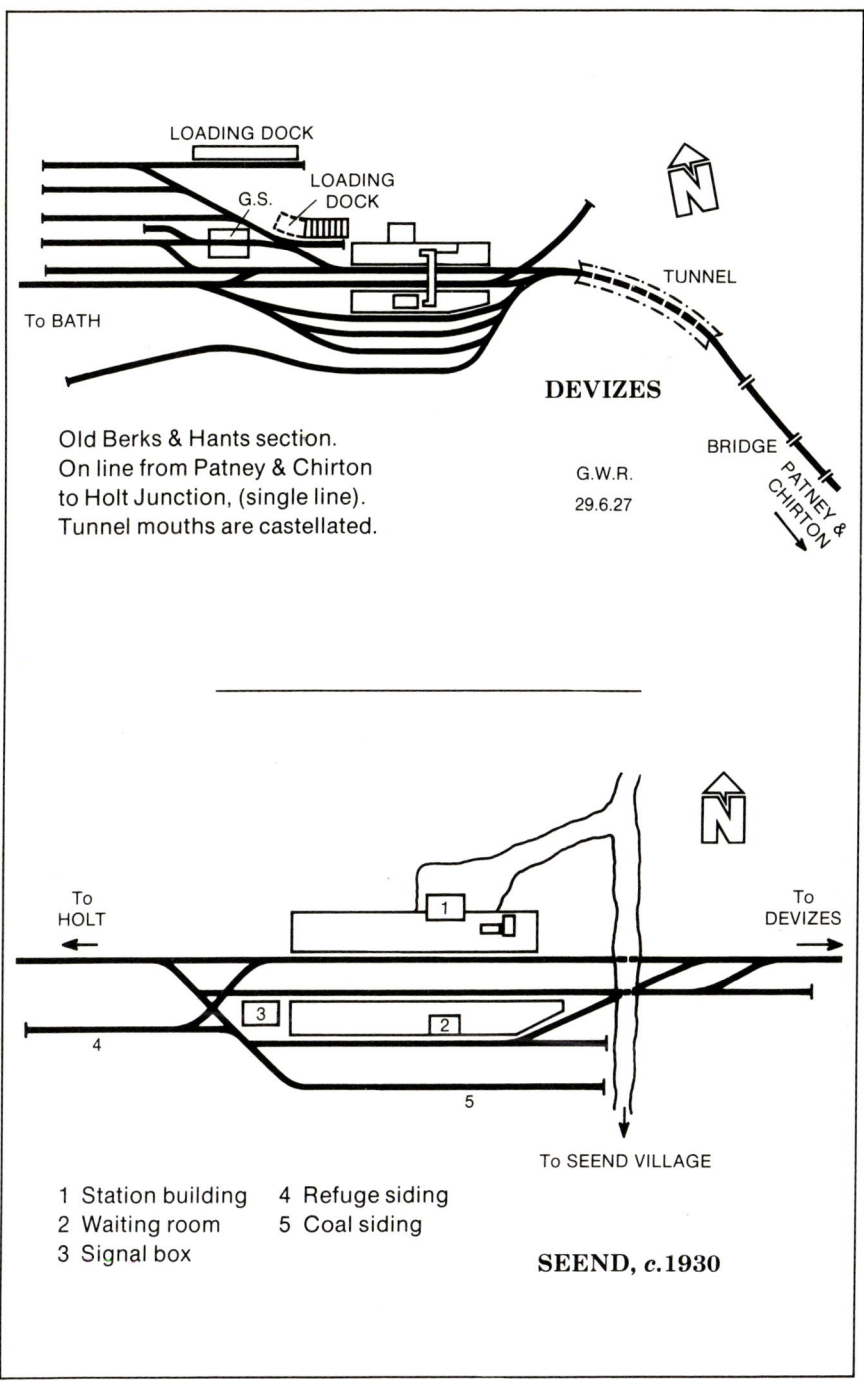

LOADING DOCK

LOADING
G.S. DOCK

DEVIZES

TUNNEL

To BATH

BRIDGE

Old Berks & Hants section.
On line from Patney & Chirton
to Holt Junction, (single line).
Tunnel mouths are castellated.

G.W.R.
29.6.27

PATNEY &
CHIRTON

To
HOLT

To
DEVIZES

1

3

2

4

5

To SEEND VILLAGE

1 Station building   4 Refuge siding
2 Waiting room   5 Coal siding
3 Signal box

SEEND, c.1930

66. Wirral Railway Circle railtour pauses at site of Holt Junction, 27 March 1971. (G. R. Hounsell)

67. Enthusiasts inspect the site of Holt Junction, 27 March 1971. The remains of the Devizes branch curves away to the right; note the wagons stored on it. (G. R. Hounsell)

Great Western Railway

NEWBURY RACES

Wednesday & Thursday, Jan. 27 & 28
EXCURSIONS TO

NEWBURY
(RACECOURSE STATION)

NOTE.—*If the Races are postponed or abandoned the special Excursion announced on this bill will not run.*

First Race, 1.30 p.m.   Last Race, 4.0 p.m.

FROM	AT	Day-Trip, Return Fares. First Class.	Third Class.	FROM	AT	Day-Trip, Return Fares. First Class.	Third Class.
	a.m.	s. d.	s. d.		a.m.	s. d.	s. d.
Weston-s.-Mare ..	9 45	17 0	10 0	Bath ..	10 55	12 0	7 3
Yatton ..	9 55	16 9	10 0	Bradford-on-			
Clevedon ..	9 35	17 0	10 0	Avon ..	11 12	10 0	6 0
Bristol—				Chippenham ..	10c 5	10 9	6 6
Bedminster ..	10 19	14 9	8 9	Melksham ..	10c25	9 6	5 9
Temple Meads ..	10 28	14 6	8 9	Trowbridge ..	11c 5	9 6	5 9
Clifton Down	9.52	15 0	9 0	Holt Junction..	11 20	8 9	5 3
Redland ..	9.54	15 0	9 0	Devizes ..	11 44	7 0	4 3
Montpelier ..	9.56	15 0	9 0				
Stapleton Road	10 17	14 9	9 0				
Lawrence Hill	10 20	14 9	8 9				

Arrive **Newbury Racecourse Station 12.30** p.m.

a Change at **Stapleton Road**
c Change at **Holt Junction**.

RETURN ARRANGEMENTS ON DAY OF ISSUE ONLY.

THE RETURN TRAIN WILL LEAVE NEWBURY RACECOURSE STATION AT **4.35** p.m. THE SAME DAY.

On the Return Journey passengers for Bristol (Temple Meads), Bedminster, Yatton, Clevedon, and Weston-super-Mare change at Lawrence Hill.

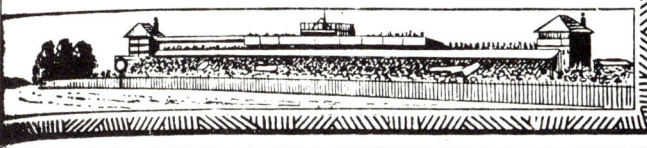

68. Poster advertising a Newbury Race Special routed via Devizes, 1926.

91

Bibliography

In addition to listed References:

To Commemorate 800 years of the Borough of Devizes, Picton Publishing, 1974.

C. Maggs, *The Bath to Weymouth Line,* Oakwood Press.

T. J. Saunders, article in *Railway Magazine,* October 1957.

Victoria County History of Wiltshire.

Cunnington Files (newspaper cuttings, etc.) in Wiltshire Archaeological & Natural History Society Library, Devizes.

B. Trigg, article in *Model Railway Constructor,* September 1965.

69. Troop train entering Devizes, probably during World War One, hauled by Midland & South Western Junction Railway 4-4-0 No. 7. (P. Strong Collection)

Printed at Picton Print
keyboarding Veronica Pinniger
page make-up Martin Dimmock
negatives Mike Simmons
litho-planning Liz Wilkins
machining Neville Fox